Field Guides to Finding a New Career

Food and
Culinary Arts

The Field Guides to Finding a New Career series

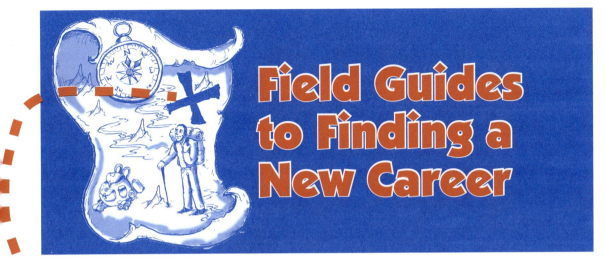

Field Guides to Finding a New Career

Food and Culinary Arts

By Ken Mondschein

Checkmark Books®
An imprint of Infobase Publishing

Field Guides to Finding a New Career: Food and Culinary Arts

Checkmark Books
An imprint of Infobase Publishing
132 West 31st Street
New York NY 10001

Library of Congress Cataloging-in-Publication Data

Mondschein, Ken.
    Food and culinary arts / by Ken Mondschein.—1st ed.
        p. cm.—(Field guides to finding a new career)
    Includes bibliographical references and index.
    ISBN-13: 978-0-8160-7599-7 (hardcover : alk. paper)
    ISBN-10: 0-8160-7599-9 (hardcover : alk. paper)
    ISBN-13: 978-0-8160-7623-9 (pbk. : alk. paper)
    ISBN-10: 0-8160-7623-5 (pbk. : alk. paper)
1. Food service—Vocational guidance—United States. 2. Hospitality industry—
    Vocational guidance—United States. I. Title.
    TX911.3.V62M65 2009
    647.95023—dc22
                                                            2008043306

Checkmark Books are available at special discounts when purchased in bulk quantities for businesses, associations, institutions, or sales promotions. Please call our Special Sales Department in New York at (212) 967-8800 or (800) 322-8755.

You can find Facts On File on the World Wide Web at http://www.factsonfile.com

Produced by Print Matters, Inc.
Text design by A Good Thing, Inc.
Illustrations by Molly Crabapple
Cover design by Takeshi Takahashi

Printed in the United States of America

Bang PMI 10 9 8 7 6 5 4 3 2 1

This book is printed on acid-free paper.

Contents

Introduction: Finding a New Career

Today, changing jobs is an accepted and normal part of life. In fact, according to the Bureau of Labor Statistics, Americans born between 1957 and 1964 held an average of 9.6 jobs from the ages of 18 to 36. The reasons for this are varied: To begin with, people live longer and healthier lives than they did in the past and accordingly have more years of active work life. However, the economy of the twenty-first century is in a state of constant and rapid change, and the workforce of the past does not always meet the needs of the future. Furthermore, fewer and fewer industries provide bonuses such as pensions and retirement health plans, which provide an incentive for staying with the same firm. Other workers experience epiphanies, spiritual growth, or various sorts of personal challenges that lead them to question the paths they have chosen.

Job instability is another prominent factor in the modern workplace. In the last five years, the United States has lost 2.6 *million jobs*; in 2005 alone, 370,000 workers were affected by mass layoffs. Moreover, because of new technology, changing labor markets, ageism, and a host of other factors, many educated, experienced professionals and skilled blue-collar workers have difficulty finding jobs in their former career tracks. Finally—and not just for women—the realities of juggling work and family life, coupled with economic necessity, often force radical revisions of career plans.

No matter how normal or accepted changing careers might be, however, the time of transition can also be a time of anxiety. Faced with the necessity of changing direction in the middle of their journey through life, many find themselves lost. Many career-changers find themselves asking questions such as: Where do I want to go from here? How do I get there? How do I prepare myself for the journey? Thankfully, the Field Guides to Finding a New Career are here to show the way. Using the language and visual style of a travel guide, we show you that reorienting yourself and reapplying your skills and knowledge to a new career is not an uphill slog, but an exciting journey of exploration. No matter whether you are in your twenties or close to retirement age, you can bravely set out to explore new paths and discover new vistas.

Though this series forms an organic whole, each volume is also designed to be a comprehensive, stand-alone, all-in-one guide to getting motivated, getting back on your feet, and getting back to work. We thoroughly discuss common issues such as going back to school, managing your household finances, putting your old skills to work in new situations, and selling yourself to potential employers. Each volume focuses on a broad career field, roughly grouped by Bureau of Labor Statistics' career clusters. Each chapter will focus on a particular career, suggesting new career paths suitable for an individual with that experience and training as well as practical issues involved in seeking and applying for a position.

Many times, the first question career-changers ask is, "Is this new path right for me?" Our self-assessment quiz, coupled with the career compasses at the beginning of each chapter, will help you to match your personal attributes to set you on the right track. Do you possess a storehouse of skilled knowledge? Are you the sort of person who puts others before yourself? Are you methodical and organized? Do you communicate effectively and clearly? Are you good at math? And how do you react to stress? All of these qualities contribute to career success—but they are not equally important in all jobs.

Many career-changers find working for themselves to be more hassle-free and rewarding than working for someone else. However, going at it alone, whether as a self-employed individual or a small-business owner, provides its own special set of challenges. Appendix A, "Going Solo: Starting Your Own Business," is designed to provide answers to many common questions and solutions to everyday problems, from income taxes to accounting to providing health insurance for yourself and your family.

For those who choose to work for someone else, how do you find a job, particularly when you have been out of the labor market for a while? Appendix B, "Outfitting Yourself for Career Success," is designed to answer these questions. It provides not only advice on résumé and self-presentation, but also the latest developments in looking for jobs, such as online resources, headhunters, and placement agencies. Additionally, it recommends how to explain an absence from the workforce to a potential employer.

Changing careers can be stressful, but it can also be a time of exciting personal growth and discovery. We hope that the Field Guides to Finding a New Career not only help you get your bearings in today's employment jungle, but set you on the path to personal fulfillment, happiness, and prosperity.

How to Use This Book

Career Compasses

Each chapter begins with a series of "career compasses" to help you get your bearings and determine if this job is right for you, based on your answers to the self-assessment quiz at the beginning of the book. Does it require a mathematical mindset? Communication skills? Organizational skills? If you're not a "people person," a job requiring you to interact with the public might not be right for you. On the other hand, your organizational skills might be just what are needed in the back office.

Destination

A brief overview, giving you and introduction to the career, briefly explaining what it is, its advantages, why it is so satisfying, its growth potential, and its income potential.

You Are Here

A self-assessment asking you to locate yourself on your journey. Are you working in a related field? Are you working in a field where some skills will transfer? Or are you doing something completely different? In each case, we suggest ways to reapply your skills, gain new ones, and launch yourself on your new career path.

Navigating the Terrain

To help you on your way, we have provided a handy map showing the stages in your journey to a new career. "Navigating the Terrain" will show you the road you need to follow to get where you are going. Since the answers are not the same for everyone and every career, we are sure to show how there are multiple ways to get to the same destination.

Organizing Your Expedition

Fleshing out "Navigating the Terrain," we give explicit directions on how to enter this new career: Decide on a destination, scout the terrain, and decide on a path that is right for you. Of course, the answers are not the same for everyone.

Landmarks

People have different needs at different ages. "Landmarks" presents advice specific to the concerns of each age demographic: early career (twenties), mid-career (thirties to forties), senior employees (fifties) and second-career starters (sixties). We address not only issues such as overcoming age discrimination, but also possible concerns of spouses and families (for instance, paying college tuition with reduced income) and keeping up with new technologies.

Essential Gear

Indispensable tips for career-changers on things such as gearing your résumé to a job in a new field, finding contacts and networking, obtaining further education and training, and how to gain experience in the new field.

Notes from the Field

Sometimes it is useful to consult with those who have gone before for insights and advice. "Notes from the Field" presents interviews with career-changers, presenting motivations and methods that you can identify with.

Further Resources

Finally, we give a list of "expedition outfitters" to provide you with further resources and trade resources.

Make the Most of Your Journey

Food is a human universal. No matter who they might be or where they might live, everybody has to eat. Furthermore, like many other human universals, food has deep resonance. Many of our first memories are of family members nurturing and feeding us. "Comfort foods" bring us both emotional succor and a sense of continuity with the past. In times of stress, one of our first reactions is often to open the refrigerator door. Likewise, the first morning cup of coffee, for many of us, is a ritual that brings sanity and order to a stressful and harried world.

Food is also linked to other meanings. Both historically and today, what one eats has marked one as a member of a social group. One important distinction is socioeconomic. In the Middle Ages, it was peasants who ate whole grains, but today, whole wheat bread is the more-expensive, healthier purchase of the middle class. The recent concern for consuming "organic" foods is another marker of class in food: Those more concerned with putting food on the table are not as concerned with its origins. The same goes for how and where one eats, as well: The Four Seasons and Tavern on the Green in New York City are seen as the ultimate in luxurious dining, while McDonald's is the province of those without resources—the economically disadvantaged person short on money, or the harried suburban soccer mom short on time.

Likewise, we instantly associate certain dishes as belonging to a certain ethnic group, or as being eaten on special occasions as a statement of group identity and common origins. Lutefisk is Swedish, lumpia is Filipino or Indonesian, latkes are Ashkenazi Jewish, and yassa is Senegalese. Food is even inseparable from religious observance: Jews eat unleavened bread to mark Passover, Muslims eat lamb on Eid al-Adha (the Feast of the Sacrifice), and the Christian sacrament of Communion, the personal experience of the divine, is received through bread and wine.

We also value food for its ability to make us whole. This goes beyond mere "comfort food" and psychological buoying: Food is also medicine. Eating the wrong foods, or not enough of the right foods, can make us ill, whether through deficiency diseases caused by a lack of certain nutrients or a surfeit of other elements. For example, scurvy is caused by a vitamin C deficiency, while too much salt intake can lead to high blood pressure. Then there are the other things we hope food will do for us:

We consume foods containing antioxidants in the hopes they will forestall cancer, or drink yerba maté and take ginkgo biloba supplements to improve our alertness and memory. It seems that every day some specious study or manufacturer's marketing campaign is extolling the virtues of some new wonder food.

Despite the hype, food-as-medicine is, in fact, a very old approach to health, dating back to the days of the ancient Greeks, where the physician's aim was to balance the patient's humors. What has changed since the past as our modern surfeit of food is seen as the cause of many ills such as obesity and high blood pressure. Accordingly, the diet industry is now a $40 billion per year concern, and weight loss has been raised to the level of a moral imperative. Dietitians and nutritionists are in demand as never before—not just in the institutional settings, such as schools and hospitals, where they have traditionally worked, but also to help private clients lose weight and live healthier lifestyles.

Despite the appeal of a home-cooked meal, Americans also spend lots of money on dining out. In 2008, the restaurant industry, according to the National Restaurant Association, was a $558 *billion* industry About 945,000 locations served 70 *billion* meals and snacks—meaning that each American eats out an average of 230 times per year. On a typical day, U.S. restaurants do one and a half billion dollars in trade. The industry is a major economic engine, employing 13.1 million people. Almost 1 out of every 10 American workers—or 9 percent of the workforce—works in the food service industry. More than half of Americans have worked in food service in some part of their careers, and for many (about one-third) it was their first job. The food service industry also provides about 4 percent of the gross domestic product. What is more, it is a secure industry: Even in times of economic slowdown, Americans still need to eat: The industry is expected to grow 4.4 percent in 2008, and add over 2 million jobs by 2010. From elegant four-star restaurants to roadside greasy spoons, the restaurant is as American as apple pie (albeit not homemade apple pie), and the food served therein is what keeps the machine of American industry running.

The restaurant industry is a very old one, beginning in the taverns of ancient Rome and the wayside inns of medieval pilgrimage routes. The restaurant as we know it today, where locals and visitors alike come to enjoy individually cooked and served meals, has its origins in eighteenth century France. The French Revolution both brought a large number of hungry provincials without family networks to Paris and left the servants of the aristocracy, trained to cook excellent food for masters who had left for safety in foreign lands, without jobs. (This history will be more fully discussed in the chapter on restaurant chefs).

However, the restaurant industry has also seen many changes in recent years. Not only are consumers demanding that it become more environmentally friendly and health-conscious, but the culture of gourmet food has become democratized. Once, *haute cuisine* was the province of a tiny population of well-off cognoscenti. Today, however, television programs such as *Top Chef* and *Emeril Live* have both educated viewers in the niceties of fine dining and the gourmet lifestyle while changing what they expect of their dining experience. Chefs such as Bobby Flay have become celebrities and household names, and the rich and famous from other walks of life are eager to cash in by investing in restaurants, or even opening their own dining establishments.

The food industry, in short, has become glamorous, and more and more people are looking for personal satisfaction in what they see as exciting, fulfilling jobs. However, only a tiny percentage of chefs ever reach the heights of an Emeril Lagasse or a Bobby Flay. Most chefs, bakers, and other food workers are not highly compensated culinary artists, but ordinary people making surprisingly little money in a very difficult industry.

Alcohol is another brave new world in food careers. Bars, taverns, and pubs have been traditional venues for socialization, business meetings, and relaxation. However, both the wine and beer industry has also benefited from an increasing consumer familiarity with, and sophistication in, their products. Every state in the union has a vintner's, and the craft-brewing revolution has changed the way Americans drink beer. "Brew pubs" and "craft" breweries now dot the American landscape. This offers both challenges to the traditional brewing industry and opportunities for those who want to make beer their livelihood. For those who see themselves on the pouring end of the distribution system, nightlife also continues to grow more sophisticated, with all varieties of drinking establishments—sports bars, fancy nightclubs, and music clubs—catering to a variety of tastes.

No matter what aspect of the culinary world you think you might enter, some advice for the career changer will always hold true. In the first place, the food service industry is *hard work*. The hours are long, the pay is usually low, and it takes time to work your way up. Working conditions are often hot and uncomfortable. Food service is also inordinately stressful; part of the job performance is handling this. (As Harry Truman said, "If you can't stand the heat, get out of the kitchen.") It is also customer-service oriented. While not every job involves being in front of the public, ultimately, everything winds up before the consumer—literally. You need to be able to take feedback and constructive criticism. Top chefs can have huge egos—you cannot. Any glory is definitely secondary to getting the job done

Secondly, what you know is *never* as important as *what you can do*. Can you chop vegetables in precisely the way you are asked to? Prepare a menu for 2,000, including vegetarian and diabetic options? Mix a perfect martini? Keep 23 orders straight? This is not a career field for those with no get-up-and go. You must be organized, motivated, and disciplined.

This is why experience is so important. No matter what you do, you are going to need experience. There is no substitute for knowing the ropes. What this means is starting at the bottom, and this means, above all else, you must be humble. If you already have experience in a related field—such as a microbiologist who is interested in becoming a brewer—that is great. However, bear in mind that there is also probably a lot you *do not* know.

Despite the performance-oriented nature of the job, there are often necessary qualifications to get a foot in the door. Chefs should have a culinary degree. Dietitians and nutritionists must be licensed. Vintners and brewers must complete apprenticeships. In other cases experience is the prime requisite: Bartending degrees are less valuable than practical experience and a work ethic for getting hired in any serious establishment.

Starting your own business is a special concern for career changers looking to enter the food industry. Many people think that starting their own brewery, wine cellar, restaurant, bakeshop, or what-have-you will be a fun and rewarding way to either escape the corporate grind or spend their retirement. Many of these entrepreneurs find themselves sorely mistaken. Some underestimate the market for their product; some simply do not have the business skills, and some are overwhelmed with the hard work for little pay that they face. Know what you are getting into, and be sure that you either have the necessary expertise, or that you know whom to ask when you need advice.

Your age, geography, and other such considerations such as your finances are also important. You are not going to have much luck growing pinot noir in Alaska, and there is not much demand for haute French cuisine in a West Virginia mining town. If you are of retirement age, this may not be the best time to start your bartending career; conversely, no one's going to take very seriously a twenty-something looking to start a vineyard with no capital.

Also think about how your career decision will affect your family and those around you: Can you pay your children's college tuition while going back to school yourself? Will a bakery bring in enough cash to make your car payments? Will your spouse or partner resent carrying more than his or her share of the mortgage? Finally, are you going to need to borrow more than you can float in order to make your business concern workable?

This volume has been carefully researched to present a balanced view of the opportunities and challenges of nine careers in what is a very difficult field. The words herein are intended not to discourage you, but to guide you toward reaching your goals and fulfillment. Keep an open mind, and above all, keep your wits about you. The food service industry can be a fascinating, creative, rewarding field. It can also be intense, frustrating, and stressful. Like everything else in the world, it is what you make of it. As always, the keys to success are to know yourself and your talents, to carefully make your plan and follow it through, and to spend your educational, social, and financial capital wisely. Be flexible, be willing to be honest with yourself—and rest assured that, with *Food and Culinary Arts* in hand, you are well-equipped to make a go of it in the exciting world of food service.

Self-Assessment Quiz

I: Relevant Knowledge

1. How many years of specialized training have you had?
   - (a) None, it is not required
   - (b) Several weeks to several months of training
   - (c) A year-long course or other preparation
   - (d) Years of preparation in graduate or professional school, or equivalent job experience

2. Would you consider training to obtain certification or other required credentials?
   - (a) No
   - (b) Yes, but only if it is legally mandated
   - (c) Yes, but only if it is the industry standard
   - (d) Yes, if it is helpful (even if not mandatory)

3. In terms of achieving success, how would rate the following qualities in order from least to most important?
   - (a) ability, effort, preparation
   - (b) ability, preparation, effort
   - (c) preparation, ability, effort
   - (d) preparation, effort, ability

4. How would you feel about keeping track of current developments in your field?
   - (a) I prefer a field where very little changes
   - (b) If there were a trade publication, I would like to keep current with that
   - (c) I would be willing to regularly recertify my credentials or learn new systems
   - (d) I would be willing to aggressively keep myself up-to-date in a field that changes constantly

5. For whatever reason, you have to train a bright young successor to do your job. How quickly will he or she pick it up?
    (a) Very quickly
    (b) He or she can pick up the necessary skills on the job
    (c) With the necessary training he or she should succeed with hard work and concentration
    (d) There is going to be a long breaking-in period—there is no substitute for experience

II: Caring

1. How would you react to the following statement: "Other people are the most important thing in the world?"
    (a) No! Me first!
    (b) I do not really like other people, but I do make time for them
    (c) Yes, but you have to look out for yourself first
    (d) Yes, to such a degree that I often neglect my own well-being

2. Who of the following is the best role model?
    (a) Ayn Rand
    (b) Napoléon Bonaparte
    (c) Bill Gates
    (d) Florence Nightingale

3. How do you feel about pets?
    (a) I do not like animals at all
    (b) Dogs and cats and such are OK, but not for me
    (c) I have a pet, or I wish I did
    (d) I have several pets, and caring for them occupies significant amounts of my time

4. Which of the following sets of professions seems most appealing to you?
    (a) business leader, lawyer, entrepreneur
    (b) politician, police officer, athletic coach
    (c) teacher, religious leader, counselor
    (d) nurse, firefighter, paramedic

5. How well would you have to know someone to give them $100 in a harsh but not life-threatening circumstance? It would have to be…
    (a) …a close family member or friend (brother or sister, best friend)
    (b) …a more distant friend or relation (second cousin, coworkers)
    (c) …an acquaintance (a coworker, someone from a community organization or church)
    (d) …a complete stranger

III: Organizational Skills

1. Do you create sub-folders to further categorize the items in your "Pictures" and "Documents" folders on your computer?
    (a) No
    (b) Yes, but I do not use them consistently
    (c) Yes, and I use them consistently
    (d) Yes, and I also do so with my e-mail and music library

2. How do you keep track of your personal finances?
    (a) I do not, and I am never quite sure how much money is in my checking account
    (b) I do not really, but I always check my online banking to make sure I have money
    (c) I am generally very good about budgeting and keeping track of my expenses, but sometimes I make mistakes
    (d) I do things such as meticulously balance my checkbook, fill out Excel spreadsheets of my monthly expenses, and file my receipts

3. Do you systematically order commonly used items in your kitchen?
    (a) My kitchen is a mess
    (b) I can generally find things when I need them
    (c) A place for everything, and everything in its place
    (d) Yes, I rigorously order my kitchen and do things like alphabetize spices and herbal teas

4. How do you do your laundry?
    (a) I cram it in any old way
    (b) I separate whites and colors

(c)   I separate whites and colors, plus whether it gets dried
(d)   Not only do I separate whites and colors and drying or non-drying, I organize things by type of clothes or some other system

5.   Can you work in clutter?
(a)   Yes, in fact I feel energized by the mess
(b)   A little clutter never hurt anyone
(c)   No, it drives me insane
(d)   Not only does my workspace need to be neat, so does that of everyone around me

IV: Communication Skills

1.   Do people ask you to speak up, not mumble, or repeat yourself?
(a)   All the time
(b)   Often
(c)   Sometimes
(d)   Never

2.   How do you feel about speaking in public?
(a)   It terrifies me
(b)   I can give a speech or presentation if I have to, but it is awkward
(c)   No problem!
(d)   I frequently give lectures and addresses, and I am very good at it

3.   What's the difference between *their, they're,* and *there*?
(a)   I do not know
(b)   I know there is a difference, but I make mistakes in usage
(c)   I know the difference, but I can not articulate it
(d)   *Their* is the third-person possessive, *they're* is a contraction for *they are*, and *there* is a deictic adverb meaning "in that place"

4.   Do you avoid writing long letters or e-mails because you are ashamed of your spelling, punctuation, and grammatical mistakes?
(a)   Yes
(b)   Yes, but I am either trying to improve or just do not care what people think

     (c)   The few mistakes I make are easily overlooked

     (d)   Save for the occasional typo, I do not ever make mistakes in usage

5.   Which choice best characterizes the most challenging book you are willing to read in your spare time?

     (a)   I do not read

     (b)   Light fiction reading such as the Harry Potter series, *The Da Vinci Code*, or mass-market paperbacks

     (c)   Literary fiction or mass-market nonfiction such as history or biography

     (d)   Long treatises on technical, academic, or scientific subjects

V: Mathematical Skills

1.   Do spreadsheets make you nervous?

     (a)   Yes, and I do not use them at all

     (b)   I can perform some simple tasks, but I feel that I should leave them to people who are better-qualified than myself

     (c)   I feel that I am a better-than-average spreadsheet user

     (d)   My job requires that I be very proficient with them

2.   What is the highest level math class you have ever taken?

     (a)   I flunked high-school algebra

     (b)   Trigonometry or pre-calculus

     (c)   College calculus or statistics

     (d)   Advanced college mathematics

3.   Would you rather make a presentation in words or using numbers and figures?

     (a)   Definitely in words

     (b)   In words, but I could throw in some simple figures and statistics if I had to

     (c)   I could strike a balance between the two

     (d)   Using numbers as much as possible; they are much more precise

4.   Cover the answers below with a sheet of paper, and then solve the following word problem: Mary has been legally able to vote for exactly half her life. Her husband John is three years older than she. Next year,

their son Harvey will be exactly one-quarter of John's age. How old was Mary when Harvey was born?

(a)   I couldn't work out the answer

(b)   25

(c)   26

(d)   27

5.   Cover the answers below with a sheet of paper, and then solve the following word problem: There are seven children on a school bus. Each child has seven book bags. Each bag has seven big cats in it. Each cat has seven kittens. How many legs are there on the bus?

(a)   I couldn't work out the answer

(b)   2,415

(c)   16,821

(d)   10,990

VI: Ability to Manage Stress

1.   It is the end of the working day, you have 20 minutes to finish an hour-long job, and you are scheduled to pick up your children. Your supervisor asks you why you are not finished. You:

(a)   Have a panic attack

(b)   Frantically redouble your efforts

(c)   Calmly tell her you need more time, make arrangements to have someone else pick up the kids, and work on the project past closing time

(d)   Calmly tell her that you need more time to do it right and that you have to leave, or ask if you can release this flawed version tonight

2.   When you are stressed, do you tend to:

(a)   Feel helpless, develop tightness in your chest, break out in cold sweats, or have other extreme, debilitating physiological symptoms?

(b)   Get irritable and develop a hair-trigger temper, drink too much, obsess over the problem, or exhibit other "normal" signs of stress?

(c)   Try to relax, keep your cool, and act as if there is no problem

(d)   Take deep, cleansing breaths and actively try to overcome the feelings of stress

3. The last time I was so angry or frazzled that I lost my composure was:
    (a) Last week or more recently
    (b) Last month
    (c) Over a year ago
    (d) So long ago I cannot remember

4. Which of the following describes you?
    (a) Stress is a major disruption in my life, people have spoken to me about my anger management issues, or I am on medication for my anxiety and stress
    (b) I get anxious and stressed out easily
    (c) Sometimes life can be a challenge, but you have to climb that mountain!
    (d) I am generally easygoing

5. What is your ideal vacation?
    (a) I do not take vacations; I feel my work life is too demanding
    (b) I would just like to be alone, with no one bothering me
    (c) I would like to do something not too demanding, like a cruise, with friends and family
    (d) I am an adventurer; I want to do exciting (or even dangerous) things and visit foreign lands

Scoring:

For each category...

For every answer of *a*, add zero points to your score.
For every answer of *b*, add ten points to your score.
For every answer of *c*, add fifteen points to your score.
For every answer of *d*, add twenty points to your score.

The result is your percentage in that category.

Chef

Career Compasses

Here's the breakdown of what it takes to become a chef.

Relevant Knowledge—not just knowing how to cook, but things like food safety and restaurant procedures (25%)

Caring about what you are doing (25%)

Organizational Skills the key to a well-run and efficient kitchen is organization (25%)

Stress Management since a kitchen is a high-stress environment (25%)

Destination: Chef

In the United States, the word *chef* is generally used to mean anyone who cooks for a living. The term is actually derived from the French *chef de cuisine*, which more or less translates to "boss of the kitchen." (*Chef* is etymologically related to the English *chief*.) Other officers traditionally report to the chef, such as the *sous*-chef (under-chef) *saucier* (in charge of sautéed items and their sauces), *pâtissier* (pastry chef) and so on, all arranged in a rigid restaurant hierarchy called the *brigade system*.

Restaurant chefs' jobs vary as much as do restaurants themselves. Modern eateries vary from informal "fill 'em and bill 'em" luncheonettes and diners to the mega-trendy eateries of New York and Los Angeles where people come as much to see and be seen as for the food. Within this spectrum, there is ample room for chefs of all stripes. The question for career changers, then, is to decide what sort of chef you want to be. Do you want to be a "celebrity chef" and cook *haute cuisine*? An executive chef for a chain? Or do you want to work outside of the restaurant system entirely, either as a personal chef delivering meals to families, companies, or other institutions, or as a private chef cooking for a single household? Your overall goals will guide what kind of culinary education you want to look into. Of course, you can become a short-order cook and go to work in the vast majority of food establishments without even needing a high school diploma. High-end cuisine, however, necessitates a degree from a culinary training institute. Generally, these take at least two years, though they can last as long as four years. You will learn everything from the correct way to chop vegetables to nutrition and food safety to how to make advanced and difficult sauces, as well as more advanced skills such as which wines to serve with which food, how to develop a menu, and the proper way to price ingredients.

Essential Gear

The chef's uniform. Every part of the chef's uniform as designed with practicality in mind. The classic chef's hat, or *toque*, is tall to allow for the circulation of air. The handkerchief was originally worn to mop sweat from one's face. The double-breasted white jacket and apron not only look clean, but repel heat and protect against burns. Chefs generally wear sturdy (even steel-toed) shoes and minimize jewelry.

As an example such a program, look at the requirements for a degree at the Culinary Institute of America (CIA) in New York, which is perhaps the best-known culinary educational institute in the United States. The CIA offers an American Culinary Federation-recognized three-tier program that includes both food- and business-related issues. These three tiers are certified culinarian, certified chef de cuisine, and certified executive chef. They also have formally accredited associate's and bachelor's degrees in culinary arts and programs in baking and pastry arts. Students must take more than 1,300 hours of hands-on training in the kitchens and bakeshops, as well as an 18-week externship and additional hours spent in the on-campus public restaurants. There are also food and wine seminars in California and Italy as well as extensive academic coursework in subjects such as the history of food. Also note that in addition to formal education as a chef, you may also need to take a municipal licensing examination. New York City, for instance, requires all "supervisors" in "food-service establishments" (which definitely describes a *chef de cuisine*) to take a 15-hour course in food hygiene and pass an exam administered by the Department of Health. If you do well in all your training, you will probably wind up as a *chef de partie*, working on one aspect of the cooking as part of a team. Only after putting significant time into this position will you begin to rise through the ranks of the brigade system. Good reviews from both the press and your superiors are the surest ways to continue advancing along this path.

Finding employment as a personal chef is more difficult in the sense that you will have to build up your own clientele and cannot rely on the traditional framework of a restaurant for job security. However, the career trajectory for a personal chef is much less stringent. There are no set educational requirements or rigid kitchen hierarchies through which to navigate. Rather, the main requisite is a demonstrated ability to prepare food for a variety of palettes with a variety of nutritional needs and deliver them in a timely fashion. Thus, many personal chefs come out of the catering field: It may be a way of focusing their business to meet the needs of a smaller number of clientele, but on a day-to-day

Essential Gear

The brigade system. The brigade system is the traditional, almost militaristic organization of the kitchen. It includes:

Chef de cuisine: The master-chef who is in charge of the kitchen. Today, one also finds executive chefs, who are in charge of the various restaurants in a chain.

Sous-chef: The under-chef.

Aboyeur: Also called an expediter, the aboyeur is in charge of taking the orders from the dining room and relaying them to the team. Also sometimes puts on the finishing touches.

Chef de partie: The "line chefs," including the saucier (sautéed items and saucer), poissonier (fish), rotisseur (roast chef), grillardin (grill chef), friturier (fried items), potager (soups), legumier (vegetables), tournant (the "roundsman" who fills in where needed), and pâtissier (pastry chef).

Commis chef: An apprentice working under a chef de partie. In the European system, this is usually, but not always, a four-year paid position.

basis. Many others simply start personal chef businesses themselves. The costs to do this are low, especially compared to starting up a restaurant, and it does not take long for word of mouth to travel if you deliver a good product. Note that a personal chef is different from a private chef, who does all the shopping, cooking, and cleanup for a single family, and may even live in their home. The job of a private chef is difficult to come by without some sort of reference or personal contact; if you feel you would be a good fit for such a position, the traditional education of the restaurant chef is your best approach.

According to the U.S. Department of Labor's Bureau of Labor Statistics, more than 3.1 million people worked as chefs and food preparation workers in the United States in 2006. Of these, 850,000 were restaurant cooks. Chefs and head cooks accounted for 115,000 workers, while only 4,900 people were private household chefs. Head chefs and those in fancy restaurants naturally tend to make the most—$60,730 in 2006 for the highest-paid 10 percent, according to the bureau. However, the median salary was $34,370, with the middle 50 percent only earning between $25,910 and $46,040 and the lowest 10 percent less than $20,160. While superstars may be able to make millions on their restaurants and marketing, most chefs are not so well paid. Restaurant chefs made a median of $20,340 in 2006, according to the bureau. Private household chefs were somewhere between the two, earning a median of $22,870.

Essential Gear

French sauces. The basis of French cuisine is the sauces, first classified by Antonin Carême in the nineteenth century. Carême based his system on four "mother sauces": *velouté*, a light stock thickened with roux, which is fried flour; *espagnole*, a sauce made from brown stock (usually veal) thickened with roux and reduced, *béchamel*, which is based on roux-thickened milk; and *allemande*, which is similar to *velouté* but thickened with egg yolk and heavy cream.

Finally, it is worth noting before embarking on this career path that work in a kitchen can be stressful and dangerous. Cooking in a restaurant environment is nothing like cooking at home. To begin with, it is hot, uncomfortable, and requires spending a lot of time on your feet. There are sharp knives, hot sauces and soups, open flames, and slippery floors. The hours can be very long, beginning with prep work in the early afternoon and lasting until 1, 2, or even 3 A.M. Though it can be an extremely rewarding career, one must go into it fully aware of all its many challenges.

You Are Here

Take stock of your own resources before starting down the path to becoming a chef.

Do you have a background in food service, nutrition, catering, or another food-related occupation? Then you are well suited to becoming a restaurant chef. Your résumé speaks for itself, since in this career experience matters more than anything else. Still, especially for higher-end jobs, you might want to consider a certificate program in culinary arts. This is especially true if your previous career was more institutional. You have the business skills. What you need now is the art.

Are you coming in from the cold? Many people every year decide to change careers to become chefs. The creative aspect of the job appeals to them, in addition to the fact that culinary schools will take people of any background. Many of these aspiring chefs quickly find that the job is not all it is cracked up to be. What they do not show you on television are all the hours of frustration, stress, and repetitive tasks. The hours are long, the work is hard, and the training is intense. Expensive culinary educations can be wasted if one is not absolutely sure that this is what one wants to do.

Organizing Your Expedition

Before you set out, know where you are going.

Decide on a destination. To become a chef, you will need a combination of formal training and practical experience. You may also decide on a sub-specialty, such as pastries. Decide exactly what you want to do: Classical French cuisine? Asian fusion? Seafood? Different schools are known for different things, and different levels of certification are needed to get your foot in the door at different levels of the restaurant world.

Scout the terrain. This is the time to look at what culinary schools are located in yourea and how much they cost. Consider taking just a weekend or evening course to get your feet wet and decide if this is what you want to do as a career. Finally, if you have your heart set on becoming

Navigating the Terrain

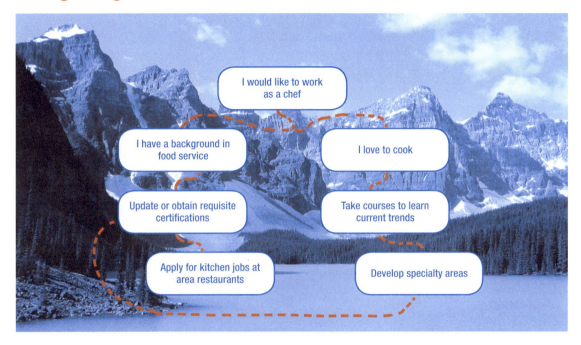

I would like to work as a chef

I have a background in food service

I love to cook

Update or obtain requisite certifications

Take courses to learn current trends

Apply for kitchen jobs at area restaurants

Develop specialty areas

a chef, look at options for financing your degree, including loans and scholarships.

Find the path that's right for you. After your education is complete (or perhaps as a part of it), you will need experience in a working kitchen. Expect to start at the bottom as a line cook. It is only with experience and practical knowledge that one works one's way up to become a top chef. Remember, the competition to get jobs at the best restaurants is intense. Also consider entering competitions to bolster your image. Cooking and baking competitions, such as those hosted by the American Culinary Federation, are becoming more and more common and drawing great amounts of attention. Winning, or even doing well, will draw attention to your work and help you build a name for yourself.

Landmarks

If you are in your twenties . . . Youth is a definite plus when becoming a chef. In fact, many restaurant chefs in the United States are in their

Notes from the Field

Nicole Pellegrino
Personal chef and caterer
New York, New York

What were you doing before you decided to change careers?

Prior to starting my own personal chef business I was an eighth-grade humanities teacher. I decided to change careers because teaching was not what I had hoped it would be. It was a heartbreaking career that I had to leave for my own sanity. Plus, I have always loved cooking and baking and throwing parties, and since I have been either working or helping others in the food service industry I thought I could probably make a lot of money if I wanted to go it alone. So I gave it a shot while bartending part-time.

Why did you change your career?

Like I said, the main reason I decided to change careers was because I couldn't sit by and watch as hundreds of students and families slipped through gaping holes in the school system. I spent a lot of time crying and feeling hopeless so I knew I had to leave and do something I loved

twenties. According to the Bureau of Labor Statistics, 37 percent are under the age of 24. (This does not differentiate between fast food workers and more upscale jobs, though.) You are also in a good position to go back to school and retool your career skills. On the minus side, expect to start at the bottom. You are less experienced and thus seen as less responsible by those in the kitchen.

If you are in your thirties or forties . . . It is not uncommon to want to become a chef in one's midcareer. It seems like an exciting, fun, and creative way out of the workday grind, and, again, television helps to sell the job. However, television never shows the large amounts of hard work, years of entry-level jobs, or low pay that are part of the field. Carefully consider your options and decide if you might want to go into another cuisine-related field such as bartender or caterer. On the plus side, you can count on being considered (whether rightly or wrongly) more responsible, and thus command more respect from your coworkers. You

and had full control over. For me the only way to ensure that things would go exactly as they should was to start up something of my own.

How did you make the transition?

Making the transition wasn't easy. I didn't have a bankroll that would allow me to quit my job and just start up my own business. I spent the summer prior to leaving teaching taking classes on catering and starting your own personal chef business; then I looked for part-time/full-time food and hospitality work. I had bartended in college so I decided to go back to bartending a few nights a week and spend the rest of the time trying to drum up business and cook for friends I could use as references. I used all the money that came in for bills, obviously, and made sure I only spent extra on business cards, flyers, food, and packaging.

What are the keys to success in your new career?

The keys to success in my current career are really the same as they are in any career. Ambition, organization, a desire to learn and grow within your industry, listening to people, caring about your product and your clients and a certain level of flexibility are all important when dealing with people and their food or anything else for that matter.

may also have the financial capital to open your own restaurant. However, a word to the wise: Just because you have the money to do something does not mean that you also have the skills or know-how.

If you are in your fifties . . . Much the same warnings that apply to midcareer changers also apply to senior employees. You will be considered more responsible, but you have less time to waste on schooling and building up experience. Consider two-year certificates instead of four-year collegiate programs. Also, be creative in your career choices! Someone who transfers to the world of cuisine from being a supplies manager for a large corporation might make a good executive chef for a large corporation. You might also consider starting your own business as a personal chef.

If you are over sixty . . . For those with an entrepreneurial spirit, becoming a chef can be a good second career. This is doubly true if you are coming from a related field (particularly a management position) and want to make use of it in the culinary world. After retiring, you may have ample free time to devote to your culinary passions, which you can grow into a business as a personal chef. Also consider investing in a restaurant, through which you can become involved in every step of the culinary process.

Further Resources

The American Culinary Association The trade organization for professional Chefs that also runs culinary competitions. http://www.acfchefs.org
The Culinary Institute of America The nation's most prestigious culinary school. http://www.ciachef.edu

Dietitian or Nutritionist

Dietitian or Nutritionist

Career Compasses

Here's the breakdown of what it takes to become a dietitian or nutritionist.

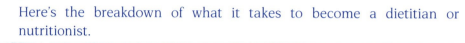

Relevant Knowledge about nutrition and human diet (30%)

Caring about your client and their needs (30%)

Organizational Skills since what this job is about is planning (30%)

Mathematical Skills since you consider food as a science—how much of which nutrients, and when (10%)

Destination: Dietitian or Nutritionist

When you come down to it, nothing is more visceral to us than food. It is more than sustenance; what we eat and how we eat it can take on an almost moralistic quality. As University of Pennsylvania psychologist Paul Rozin and French sociologist Claude Fischle found in a 2003 study, while the French associate chocolate cake with the word "celebration," Americans are more likely to say "guilt." Television, movies, and magazines tell us that thin people are classy and beautiful; conversely, fat people are

12

seen as lacking the self-discipline necessary to live a happy, productive life. What is more, the American diet is considered by many people to be profoundly disordered. There is no doubt that we are experiencing an epidemic of overabundance, and countless studies have sought to find out why 30 percent of the U.S. population is obese. None of them have produced any definite answers. The only thing that is certain is that the diet industry itself has become a multibillion-dollar business. We are willing to spend endless amounts of money to become thinner, no matter how fraudulent or dangerous the method.

It is because of these facts that dietitians and nutritionists are needed more than ever. Dietitians and nutritionists are the professionals who scientifically study and regulate the human diet. They use their findings to promote good health through sound eating choices. This may be done therapeutically, such as designing a menu to help an obese person lose weight, or preventatively, such as ensuring that children in underprivileged households do not develop nutritional deficiencies. It may also be done administratively, such as running the kitchen of a hospital or other large institution.

The approach of the dietitian or nutritionist is, in reality, a very old approach to health. As medieval physicians lacked modern surgical or diagnostic tools, as well as antibiotics and anesthesia, their medical practices were holistic and preventative rather than diagnostic and curative. Drawing on medical treatises written by their Greek and Roman forebears, they constructed an elaborate dietary science. Foods were grouped according to different natural qualities: cinnamon was warming, for instance, while melons were cold and wet. Balance was essential. For example, it was dangerous for someone who was phlegmatic to partake of cold and wet foods. Food was thus both a means of sustenance and a means of preserving life and redressing imbalances. "Let food be your medicine and medicine be your food," as the ancient Greek physician Hippocrates was held to have said.

Today, thanks to the work of generations of food scientists, we divide nutrients into several groups: carbohydrates, fats, and proteins; fiber (indigestible material, necessary for healthy digestive functioning); minerals and vitamins (about 12 of each are characterized as "essential"); and water (without which no life can survive). Dietitians and nutritionists must know the importance of each and how it works in the body. They utilize this knowledge to help balance the food intake of patients in a

Essential Gear

Nutrients. Nutrients are divided into two groups: *Macronutrients* (those we need large quantities of) and *micronutrients* (those trace minerals we need to support metabolism). The key macronutrients are *carbohydrates*, which we burn for energy and are made up of sugars; *proteins*, which are necessary for muscle metabolism and are made up of amino acids; and *fats*, which can be burned for energy but are also necessary to support our cellular metabolism. (The reason why fatty things "taste good" is because our ancestors increased their odds of staying alive by eating as much as possible. Fat has more than twice as many calories—9 kilocalories per gram—as proteins and carbohydrates, which have 4 kilocalories per gram.)

Of the minerals we consume, sodium chloride (that is, ordinary table salt), magnesium, and potassium are all necessary for the nervous system. Calcium also makes up our bones. Minerals such as phosphorus, magnesium, iodine, iron, and zinc are all very important and usually work together with enzymes in cellular metabolism. Deficiencies of any of these elements can result in disease. In fact, many of their nutritional functions were discovered by scientists looking for cures for deficiency diseases. *Vitamins* are a diverse group of substances that includes any organic compound required for life that cannot be synthesized within the body. Finally, sufficient water is, of course, also necessary to live!

variety of settings, from hospitals to nursing homes to the practices of doctors or other health professionals.

Many also work in schools, prisons, or other institutions. Some work for food manufacturers, analyzing, reporting on, and making suggestions to improve their product. Still others are engaged primarily on the research end.

Each of these dietitians goes by a different name within the field. A *clinical dietitian* works with patients in health-care facilities. Like any other health-care provider, they see what each individual patient's needs are, provide a nutrition program, and evaluate the results. Some have specialties, such as working with overweight patients, diabetics, those with renal (kidney) failure, or the elderly. *Community dieticians* are public health workers, looking more at prevention and the large trends of diet and health. They work with both individuals and groups to improve quality of life, and may be based in public health clinics, home-care agencies, or not-for-profit agencies. *Management dietitians* also deal with the big picture. They may handle the budgeting and planning for large facilities such as company cafeterias, prisons, or universities, and may supervise many clinical dietitians. In addition, they are usually also responsible for maintaining hygiene and sanitary conditions, as well buying equipment and supplies. Finally, *consultant dietitians* work for private clients, either individuals or organizations, ranging from sports teams to restaurants to supermarkets to agribusinesses.

Your path to becoming a dietitian or nutritionist always begins with formal education. Most states require you to have at least a bachelor's degree in dietetics, nutrition, food service management, or another such area. Most states and jurisdictions also have strict licensing and certification requirements. In fact, 35 require licenses, 12 require government certification, and one requires registration. What this means in practical terms is that you will have to pass a government-administered training program and examination. The American Dietetic Association also awards a Registered Dietitian credential to dietitians who pass an exam after finishing their coursework and an internship; such dietitians must also take 75 hours of coursework every five years to maintain their certification.

According to the U.S Bureau of Labor Statistics, there were some 57,000 dietitians and nutritionists working in the United States as of 2006. More than half worked in the health care field, such as in hospitals or nursing homes. Others worked in public institutional settings such as public health or correctional facilities. Some worked in colleges and universities, for airlines, for company cafeterias, or anywhere where food had to be prepared *en masse*. Additionally, some worked as *sports nutritionists*, employed by everyone from individual "weekend warriors" to Olympic teams to help them eat right for the challenges of their particular sport. The median salary for that year was $46,980. The top 10 percent made more than $68,330, while the middle 50 percent made between $38,430 and $57,090 and the lowest 10 percent made less than $29,860. Those who earned the most tended to work as consultants, in management, in education and research, and outpatient care centers or hospitals. The employment outlook is expected to be good, though it is threatened by two dangers: less qualified workers may be employed instead of trained and licensed dietitians and nutritionists, and insurance agencies may decide to not cover their services.

You Are Here

Take stock of your own resources before starting down the path to becoming a dietitian or nutritionist.

Do you have a background in food service, catering, or another food-related occupation? In this case, you have some great advantages. You are used to dealing with food in an analytic way: costs, balance, and the logistics of serving it are all familiar to you. However, you must now learn to examine food in a scientific way, with an eye toward the health of your clients. Those hors d'oeuvres that your catering clients raved about might be high enough in sodium to kill a horse. This is why dietitians and nutritionists must attend rigorous programs that train them to analyze food and see what is best for the needs of individual clients.

Are you a health care professional? Again, you have a great advantage. Not only do you probably have the basics of nutritional science under your belt, but you are used to looking at things from the perspective of your patients. Now you must deepen your knowledge of nutrition, hone the analytical skills necessary to plan out long-term diets, and learn the logistical, business-side of the profession with things like budget planning.

Are you deficient in vitamin E (experience)? Not to worry! Dietitian and nutritionist training programs are comprehensive. Your professors will take you through all you need to know, from vitamin A to zinc. Commit yourself to learning, and you will not go wrong.

Organizing Your Expedition

Before you set out, know where you are going.

Decide on a destination. No matter where you are coming from, you need education or certification to become a dietitian or nutritionist. Look at your state's laws! What are the requirements in terms of academic qualifications, testing, and certification? How can you best fulfill

Navigating the Terrain

I would like to work as a dietitian or nutritionist

Research dietitian and nutritionist programs in your area

Go back to school and complete necessary certification

Get experience through internships and volunteering, if necessary

Apply for jobs

them? Regardless of how much you believe you know through independent study, all dietitians must complete these necessary requirements.

Scout the terrain. After looking at your state's requirements, seek out schools in your area. No matter where you live, it is likely there is a dietitian or nutritionist program nearby. There were 281 bachelor's of science programs and 22 master's programs in 2007 that were approved by the American Dietetic Association's Commission on Accreditation for Dietetics Education.

Find the path that's right for you. After your formal education is over, more work might need to be done. The more experience you have, the better. Look for internships and volunteer opportunities with such places as nursing homes, hospitals, community health initiatives, and not-for-profits to use as résumé-builders. Depending on where you are, clinical practice hours may also be part of your certification requirements.

Notes from the Field

Katie Sobel
Food consultant, health counselor, and health-supportive personal chef
New York, New York

What were you doing before you decided to change careers?

Before I decided to make a career shift, I was working full time in daytime television as part of the production team on a very successful morning talk show. In that time, I did everything from research entertainment and news stories, edit and produce video content, book experts, produce segments and fact check. However, even then, I found myself eagerly pitching the health and food topics or contributing on those particular segments.

Why did you change your career?

I changed careers because I felt that I was only touching the tip of the iceberg with my true potential and that I wanted to spend more time learning and growing in a community that represented more of my true passion. After working in the entertainment community for nearly six years, I realized that I could invest in myself as the "product" and not just experience the content from the outside prospective that is more common to the producer role. However, I very much have the big picture mindset of a producer and am a great idea generator. I realized that by mixing my "producer" skills together with my education in nutrition and the culinary arts I'd have that much more to contribute. I like to think that I became embedded—and now have a unique inside perspective. My intention moving forward in my career is to continue to fuse together my media background with my passion for health, food, and sustainability within our food system and our bodies.

How did you make the transition?

Although I knew I was interested in exploring the food world, my transition out of TV was something that took place slowly over about a year and half. Initially, I began my quest for knowledge by enrolling at the Institute for Integrative Nutrition (IIN) here in New York City. It was there that I learned over 100 dietary theories under the guidance of leading experts like Dr. Andrew Weil, Deepak Chopra, Marion Nestle, and Dr. Mehmet Oz. In the end, I became a board-certified holistic health counselor through the American Association for Drugless Practitioners

(AADP). I was profoundly moved by that experience and used my knowledge as a platform for growth into the next phase of my education. Luckily, IIN was a part-time program and it allowed me to maintain my work in television. However, my gut knew that this next step would be most beneficial if I were able to fully submerge myself in the academic experience and truly be focused on my studies. I was accepted to NYU's master's in food studies but in the end decided to attend culinary school at the Natural Gourmet Institute for Health and Culinary Arts. I knew that there I would really learn application and hands-on skills and not just food from a theoretical point of view. Natural Gourmet is one of the only schools of its kind that explores diet and health from a whole foods approach with an emphasis on a plant based diet and local, seasonal, organic and sustainable choices. Upon completion of my chef's training program I did a couple internships and began looking for paid work as a personal chef, consultant, and health counselor.

What are the keys to success in your new career?

I have learned that when you are creating a niche, you have to be very, very fluid but focused. You cannot rely on other people finding "a place for you" or even flipping open the newspaper and finding a job that is the right match. It is really a matter of slowly narrowing in on where you want to grow and contribute and reaching out to as many outlets that you think represents those areas of interest. Given my unique background and credentials, it has not been difficult for me to catch the attention of prospective employers—however, it is a bit more challenging to have them create a position for you that does not already exist per se. My advice is to attend every networking event you can find, bring business cards, volunteer and communicate. When you are making a big career change and you are several years out of school or more, often times your daily setting, social group, and contacts are limited to the people in your current profession. You really have to put yourself out there because the face-to-face contact and real life energy is invaluable. I suggest that even if you are thinking that something is an itch or just a hobby, start to pursue it now. Join that club, attend that workshop, visit that location. It is never too early to build those connections and at the same time explore a passion that may eventually become your new career.

Landmarks

If you are in your twenties . . . Congratulations! You have your whole career ahead of you, and this is an excellent time to go back to school to become a dietitian or nutritionist. Remember that you may have to begin in low-level positions and work under the supervision of others before you can become a managing dietitian or nutritionist for a large institution. Build on your interests. If you are a former semi-professional athlete or competitive runner, for instance, think about going into the world of sports nutrition.

If you are in your thirties or forties . . . Because of the extensive training and discipline required of dietitians and nutritionists, older workers are in a good position to transition into the field. Additionally, if your children are old enough to take care of their own basic needs, this is a good time to go back to school. Management experience is a definite plus. Many of your day-to-day life skills—making budgets, organizing schedules, and taking care of bills—also transfer to becoming a dietitian or nutritionist. You may be in a strong enough position financially to look into starting your own business as a consulting dietitian, or even combine the career with that of personal chef to start your own home-nutrition service.

If you are in your fifties . . . There is no reason why a senior employee career changer cannot become a dietitian or nutritionist. For those who have spent their careers in food service, obtaining certification in this field might, in fact, be a logical step toward promotion. You can then use this position as a bridge job to change to becoming a full-time dietitian or nutritionist. Much as with career changers in their thirties and forties, you might also have the know-how and resources to start your own business. You are likely to have a wealth of contacts and resources in your own community to help you get started.

If you are over sixty . . . The senior citizen community is one of the groups in greatest need of dietitians and nutritionists. As such, you are in a prime position to understand and meet the needs of this market. While your age may give some people pause at hiring you (though not so much at geriatric-care or nursing facilities), you should also consider volunteering your services or, like younger career changers, starting your own business.

Further Resources

American Dietetic Organization The professional organization for dietitians, offering certification, training, and advocacy. http://www.eatright.org

National Organization of Sports Nutrition Helping those who help athletes reach their peak potential. http://www.nasnutrition.com

Caterer

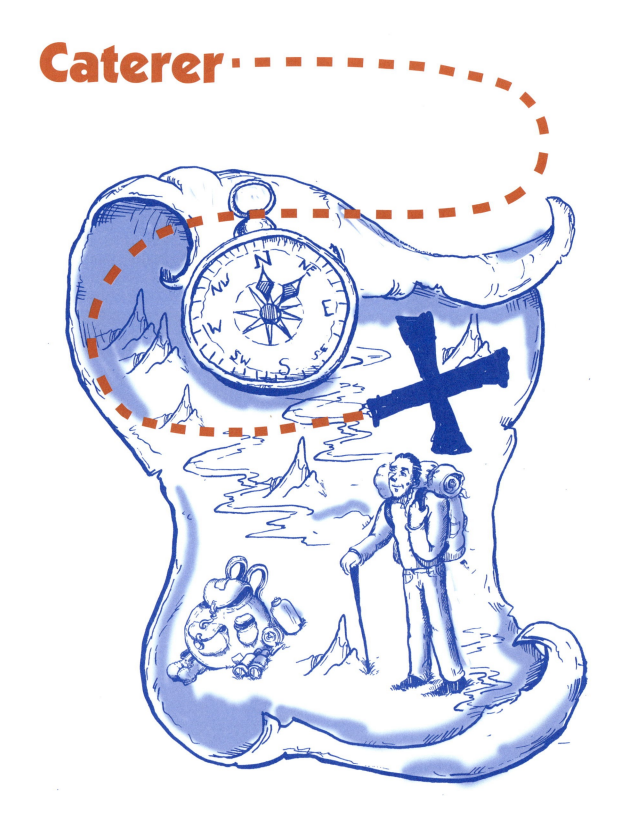

Caterer

Career Compasses

Here's the breakdown of what it takes to become a caterer.

Relevant Knowledge about cooking, budgeting, and how to plan out jobs (20%)

Caring about your clients, what they want, and their needs (20%)

Organizational Skills since your profit margin depends on planning out menus, budgeting, and keeping your staff organized (40%)

Stress Management especially during chaotic catering events (20%)

Destination: Caterer

In its simplest form, catering is the service of providing food and beverages at a remote site. Among other things, it can be a picnic meal, hors d'oeuvres and drinks at a reception, a self-serve buffet, or a five-course, sit-down dinner. The food might be made on-site, or prepared in a different location and transported. Caterers are also in charge of serving drinks, from canned soda and bottled water to elaborate bar schemes featuring fountains, trained bar staff, and exotic mixed drinks. Caterers are increasingly becoming full-service agencies that arrange events like multimedia performances to please all of the guests' senses. They may coordinate lighting, place settings, and even music. The aim is not just to delight the clients with novelty and luxury, but to provide the desired ambiance: celebratory for a stage-of-life event such as wedding, energetic for a product launch, relaxed for a retirement party, or low-key and cordial for a business meeting or trade convention.

Caterers work for a variety of clients and in many situations. Some provide mobile catering for remote locations. An example of this is the *craft services* caterer who brings food for cast and crew to movie sets. Others work for banquet halls, private clubs, and other facilities where people might hold events such as weddings. Some are employed by the venue, some have exclusive contracts, and some must actually pay the location a portion of what they receive from the client. Still others work for subdivisions of larger food-service companies in places such as dining halls of colleges and universities. Finally, some caterers specialize in providing lunches or dinners to corporate events.

Caterers can come from a variety of backgrounds. Many begin as professional chefs, event planners, or meeting facilitators.

Essential Gear

Hors d'oeuvres is French for "outside the work," meaning "outside" the main work of preparing the meal. They are essential to the caterer's trade, as they are easy to prepare in large amounts, easy to serve, and require little cleanup. A few classics are:

A **canapé,** French for "couch," is a tiny open-faced sandwich on a cracker, puff pastry, or (traditionally) stale white bread that has been toasted, sautéed, or fried and topped with something spicy or salty. They are served with drinks—which is a good thing, since they are designed to make one thirsty!

A **vol-au-vent** ("windblown" in French) is a small, hollow piece of puff pastry that can be stuffed with a savory filling. A similar concept is the **barquette** ("little boat"), which is shaped like a little ship and filled with savory filling.

Smörgåsbord, in Swedish, means something like "sandwich table" and is traditional during Christmas gatherings (*Julbord,* or "Yule table"). It consists of both cold and hot dishes. In keeping with Sweden's nautical heritage, it usually includes many types of fish.

Others are simply creative individuals who see an opportunity for them to apply their culinary skills. The main requirement is good business sense. Outside of the fundamentals of cooking and serving food, as well as the basics of food safety, caterers must know how to estimate and work within budgets, hire and supervise staff, and plan everything out in a detailed and efficient manner. All of this requires discipline and organizational skills. However, it is often a caterer's artistic flair, creativity, and individuality that really makes the event special. Catering is thus a mixture of art and science.

Any catering job begins by dialoguing with the client to see what his or her needs are. Does he or she want a specific theme? Are there any dietary preferences or requests? Responding to a client's wishes is a hallmark of a good caterer. The next step is determining the budget and figuring out what to charge. Generally, caterers charge on a per-person basis, sometimes with a minimum price. Consider how long you will be working and how much additional staff you will need. A sit-down dinner, for example, will require much more staff, since there is much more to do: twice the china, and usually three courses and coffee. Also, of course, you will need to consider the cost of the food and beverages you plan to use, as well as the miscellaneous expenses for things like decorations. Besides all of this, there is also the red tape to deal with. Permits are necessary to run a catered affair and often cost additional money. If liquor is to be served, you must comply with certain state and local regulations. Caterers must also usually have business licenses and regular health inspections, which vary by jurisdiction. This is the difference between a legitimate caterer and a fly-by-night operation.

With all of this in mind, you can get an idea of all the work it takes to be a caterer. The hours can be long and difficult, often beginning with preparation work early in the morning and ending with cleanup late into night. Weekend work is more the rule than the exception. Nonetheless, it can be a rewarding career. The Bureau of Labor Statistics does not keep track of the salaries of caterers working in the United States, but a comparison with private household chefs might be informative. Such workers made a median of $22,870, with the middle 50 percent earning between $17,960 and $31,050, the lowest 10 percent earning less than $14,690 and the highest 10 percent more than $55,040. Of course, those who own their own business make the lion's share of the profit, while low-level employees tend to make less.

To change career tracks to become a caterer, you must ask some basic questions. The first is if you want to work for yourself or for a company or catering venue. Working for an employer has its advantages, such as not having to assume financial risk, more regular hours, and possibly health care and other benefits. The downside is that such businesses may also be looking for someone with proven experience in cuisine or food-service management. In such a case, it would be better to go back to school to earn the necessary certification. Seeking such a position might also involve taking low-level bridge jobs until you have earned the necessary experience. For those without enough money to go into business themselves, this may be the only possible career path.

Though working for an established company has its advantages, many people prefer the thrill, and the attendant responsibility, of working for themselves. Because so many caterers are self-employed, and because catering gigs come both large and small, this is an easier career move than most. The important thing is to work your network of contacts in order to get as much business as possible, and to get the word out about your services. Also make sure you have enough start-up capital to buy the equipment you need and to pay your initial expenses. Start small, and do not get in over your head with elaborate preparations before you have the necessary experience. Finally, find a business mentor to loan you much-needed experience. You want to know what you are getting into. (For more tips, see our appendix on starting your own business.)

You Are Here

Take stock of your own resources before starting down the path to becoming a caterer.

Do you have a background in cooking or food? Then you are ahead of the game. Culinary schools, dietitian programs, and the like teach you not only about food, but also planning. Most of what catering is about is organization, budgeting, and keeping things flowing. You will also be familiar with sanitary and other food service regulations. Add a familiarity with the culinary arts, and you have a winning combination. If you are still lacking some element of the catering formula, consider hiring an employee or partnering with someone who completes the mix.

Do you have a background in business? This is almost as good as a background in the culinary industry. Again, catering is a detailed, numbers-oriented *business* before it is about the guests' pleasure. However, despite your business acumen, you may lack certain skills, whether culinary, decorative, or otherwise. Fortunately, money can make up for a lot of short-comings, in that you can hire cooks and designers. What money cannot make up for is poor planning or lack of vision. Take special care with the planning and pricing of your affairs. If you really want to know all aspects of the business (or plan on doing it all yourself), then you might want to consider some courses to make up for your deficiencies.

Are you still trying to get on the guest list? Then start learning! Cooking can be learned; many culinary schools offer courses in cooking, and recipes can be scaled up to party-sizes. In the same way, budgeting and price-estimating skills can be acquired. The trick is not to run head-on into a steep learning curve. That salmon mousse that your dinner guests always think is so delicious just might not be practical or economic to cook for a crowd of 300! Also consider getting a part-time job or even volunteering your services in order to learn the ropes. Cooking for church groups and community organizations can be a good way to gain experience and get a foot in a door. Start small and work your way up.

Navigating the Terrain

Notes from the Field

Aja Tahari Marsh
Caterer
New York, New York

What were you doing before you decided to change careers?

I'd worked at a small catering company in college, where I was studying photography, design, and journalism. I wasn't totally sure I wanted to do only those things for a living, and it wasn't until a friend of mine mentioned she was interested in going to culinary school that I realized cooking for a living was a viable option. While still in college and afterward, I moved to New York and I did some work in photography—headshots, production stills, press photos, and personal travel and portraiture projects. I also did some design for logos, business cards, postcards, CDs, Web sites, and posters. Most of this was through friends, friends-of-friends, or colleagues. But because that wasn't taking up all of my time, I also job-hopped. From working as the marketing and promotions director of a non-profit theater company to working the 4 A.M. baking shift at a catering company to hostessing and waiting tables.

Why did you change your career?

After awhile I grew bored of working front of house at a restaurant. It was fun while it lasted, but I needed something a bit more stimulating. I looked into culinary school at the Natural Gourmet Institute, but wasn't sure I wanted to take the financial plunge of the Chef's Training Program. After toying with the idea of just taking public classes at various cooking schools in the city, I just decided to go for it. I took out a loan, quit my job, and went to natural cooking school for four and a half months.

Being a vegetarian at the time, I was greatly attracted to this school because it focused on vegan, organic, and natural cooking, as well as the healing properties of food—all of this greatly appealed to me and I wanted to learn as much about it as I could. I'd always enjoyed my experiences at my catering jobs, and would often throw elaborate dinner parties at my home, and I loved the idea of nourishing people with healthy and exciting food. Natural Gourmet armed me with many of the tools I needed to launch myself to the next level, and work for myself—which has always been something I'd prefer to do.

How did you make the transition?

Well, I guess since I wasn't well established before, it wasn't too hard to make the transition. What was more difficult was how to get started. If I was going to be a personal chef, I had to have clients to survive. I took a part-time job in the kitchen of a haute vegetarian restaurant in NYC and while I did not mind the long hours, and the pay was measly, I withered without the interaction with the people who were eating food I carefully prepared with my hands. After a few months there, glad for the experience, I decided enough was enough, and quit that job, and took a risk, hoping a client, or some other freelance work would come. And so it did.

While my clients are not all super long-lasting, now one job usually melds into the next, and I not only get referrals through NGI, but I also am now getting more word-of-mouth clients by doing small catering jobs. I love the personal chef work, because it allows for a lot of interaction with clients who all have unique tastes and dietary concerns. It keeps me on my toes because every client is a new and different challenge, and all of my creative and artistic interests are still very much at play.

While catering is more of a secondary aspect to my career, mostly because I do not have my own facilities so am better capable of handling small or private in-home events, it is something that I always enjoy because the menus are more reflective of my personality and the food I like to cook—more so than with my personal cooking clients, who I usually have to accommodate more specifically.

What are the keys to success in your new career?

For me, I'd say patience is key. As is persistence. As is the ability to "weather the storms" as they come. There are some weeks and months where I am getting more work than I can accept, and other times with hardly any work at all. It balances out in the end, but I have to be prepared to work very hard when the tide comes in so that I can maintain myself when it goes out. Because sometimes a client decides to go out of town, or realizes they no longer need your services, and I'm always looking for other little jobs, usually short-term or one-off opportunities like cooking classes, food demonstrating, or non-food related gigs—they help to fill in the gaps, and introduce me to new circles of people, who, you never know, may be able to use my culinary skills in the future for an event.

Organizing Your Expedition

Before you set out, know where you are going.

Decide on a destination. Several things are needed to become a caterer, including chops in the kitchen, organizational skills, and business acumen. You must also decide if you want to work for other people or go into business for yourself. Take stock of what you have on the menu. What capital do you bring to the table, both in terms of skills and financial resources?

Scout the terrain. The task now is to compensate for whatever areas in which you might be deficient. If you do not have money for starting your own business, or if you are inexperienced, consider working for someone else for a while, or at least starting small. If you do not have culinary expertise, hire or partner with a chef or taking cooking courses. If it is business sense you lack, it is possible to take courses in this, as well—and, of course, experience is always the best teacher.

Find the path that's right for you. If you are going into business for yourself, you need to answer several more questions. Who is your market? What sort of events will you cater? What services will you provide? A viable business plan is the heart of any successful venture. Investigate the needs of groups in your community that may use catering services. Take informal surveys, perhaps with other caterers, of what has and has not worked in the past before venturing into the marketplace.

Landmarks

If you are in your twenties . . . If you are in your twenties, your main problem is likely a lack of capital and/or experience. However, this is easily rectified: work for other people! Not only will you gain valuable knowledge of the way a catering business is run, but you will make important contacts to help you on your way. Continue to work independently honing your own culinary skills.

If you are in your thirties or forties . . . The path for midcareer changers depends on your personality type. Are you an organizational person? An artistic designer? A hard-headed businessperson? Exploit your strengths by understanding how they could fit into a caterer's business plan. Career changers of this age also begin to gain the confidence and wherewithal to start their own businesses.

If you are in your fifties . . . Age discrimination is an unfortunate reality. However, the great thing about becoming a caterer is that so many caterers are self-employed, leaving little room for ageism of any sort. Senior career changers usually have a wealth of experience (if not actual money) to draw upon. Work your contacts, as well. You can gain an "in" catering events for businesses and organizations with which you have a history.

If you are over sixty . . . As they say in the advertising business, capitalize on your market positioning! Who would not want some homemade comfort food from Nana's Catering? Much as with senior career changers, second-career starters have nothing holding them back from catering success. Start with catering an organization you are part of, find what contacts you can, and work outward from there.

Further Resources

***The Everything Guide to Starting and Running a Catering Business* by Joyce Weinberg** Weinberg runs the novice through everything from economics to obtaining necessary licenses.
National Restaurant Association The restaurant industry's trade organization. The Web site is a great resource, including many terrific, informative, and free articles on running a catering business. http://www.restaurant.org
Caterer.com Find a job in catering, hire someone, or use the salary calculator. Also chock full of useful advice. http://www.caterer.com

Food Stylist

Food Stylist

Career Compasses

Here's the breakdown of what it takes to become a food stylist.

Relevant Knowledge of the tricks of the trade and relevant laws (60%)

Caring about your job (10%)

Organizational Skills since photo shoots are no time to dilly-dally (20%)

Stress Management since the job can be hectic (10%)

Destination: Food Stylist

Ever hear the expression, "You can practically taste it with your eyes?" In the world of food advertising, the eyes are all you have to make the sale. Every day, we are bombarded with pictures featuring delicious-looking food. But why does our coffee never look so deliciously foamy? Why does the syrup never glisten so on our pancakes? Why is our ice cream never so perfectly scooped? And why do our hamburgers never come on such ideal sesame-seed buns? Perhaps it is because the coffee has a teaspoon of soap added to it, the syrup is actually motor oil, the ice cream is mostly shortening, and the bun had each of the sesame seeds individually added with a dollop of glue. The person responsible for all this magic—or trickery—is the food stylist.

The somewhat offbeat, but still fascinating, world of the food stylist lies at the intersection of cooking and art. The job of a food stylist is to make food look good for the camera—a task which, much like making a human model look perfect, requires a degree of subterfuge. Not only does a camera "see" differently from the human eye, but food does not look its best under bright studio lights—in fact, it may look positively hideous. Thus, food stylists employ a number of tricks, such as the aforesaid soap-in-the-coffee, vegetable-shortening faux ice cream, and hand-glued sesame seeds. At their best, food stylists can give you an idea of what something is supposed to smell and taste like, exciting the pleasure centers of the human brain and giving you the urge to immediately run out and buy the product.

Essential Gear

Make the pizza shine. Why does your pizza never get those strings of cheese like in the ads? Obviously, because when you cut a slice, you also cut through the cheese. To get that mouth-watering, runny-cheese effect, bake the pizza halfway and then cut one slice out. Add extra cheese around the cut, finish baking, and then take your pictures as you lift the extra-cheesy pizza slice.

Food stylists work under a number of constraints. The first and foremost is legal: the U.S. government requires that food photographed for advertisements be that which the consumer can actually buy. (Cookbooks and magazines, however, have no such mandates.) The art, then, lies in showing the fantasy of juicy flame-broiled burgers with crispy green lettuce instead of grey, slimy fast-food burgers with wilted greens. The food might have things done to it that you would never want done to something you would eat—glazing with wood varnish, grilling with a clothes iron, or spraying with chemicals are just three possible tricks. Other constraints are related to the nature of the industry, such as time and budget. Photography sessions and studio space are expensive. A good food stylist is also a good planner, organizing and getting things done in an efficient fashion, and usually doing a lot of preparation work before a shoot even begins.

The food stylist, like the rest of the creative team, should arrive at the place for the shoot before the client does. The shoot will be taking place on the client's dime, and he or she generally wants to see things go as quickly, efficiently, and cost-effectively as possible. A stand-in for the food should already be prepared out of the faux-food materials, unless, of course, the client specifically asked you not to make one. (When in doubt, make a stand-in: time is more valuable than materials.) The stand-in must match the size, shape, color, texture, and surface composition of the target food (also known as the "hero" of the shoot). Having the stand-in will help the photographer make decisions about lighting and composition without worrying about the "hero" melting, dissolving, or losing its shape on set. Following these test shots, construction of the "hero" food can begin. This is where the artistic side of the process comes in. Everything must be *better* than real life. To shoot a bowl of cereal, for instance, dozens of boxes must be opened, the most ideal flakes extracted individually with medical tweezers and inserted into a bowl of carefully prepared milk-substitute (or several, depending on how long the shoot will go and how well the food holds up). Tablecloths must be ironed with perfect creases, silverware must be spot-free, and the slightest grain of pollen must be cleaned off the glassware with sticky tape. Attention to detail is of the utmost importance.

Essential Gear

Keep the spuds handy, or loads of ice cream. Ice cream has the unfortunate tendency to melt under hot studio lights. Thankfully, mashed potatoes treated with food coloring or a stiff mixture of shortening and sugar can substitute in some circumstances. If you are shooting for advertising, things get tricky because, by law, you have to use the real thing. Also, mashed potatoes just do not look like premium ice cream. Better have a lot of the real stuff around, and freeze it rock-solid.

To become a food stylist, it is helpful, but not essential, to have a background in photography or cooking. While you might think that food stylists are exclusively employed in advertising industry-heavy cities such as New York and Los Angeles, they are actually employed all over the country. However, because the smaller companies located outside of major metropolitan areas simply do not have the budget or resources for a full-crew shoot, one person has to suffice to do the jobs of food stylist, photographer, and lighting specialist. Some food stylists therefore double as photographers—or, perhaps more accurately, some photographers double as food stylists. This can be a very good way to get your foot in the door to the food styling world, especially if you are already an established commercial photographer.

For those going directly into food styling from another career, learning the job (and making the necessary contacts) is a process of apprenticeship. Fledgling food stylists will often "shadow" and assist an established food stylist, learning tricks of the trade as they go. Generally, to win an assistant position, it helps to have a culinary background. Remember that, as with all creative jobs, evaluation of your abilities is subjective. Your portfolio is everything. Make sure to develop a stunning collection of your work over a wide variety of subject matter. It does not have to be specific to food—your potential mentor is looking to see a sharp eye for detail and an inclination for composition and design. Networking is also critical to gaining employment in this field. Show your portfolio to multiple people, collect positive recommendations, and take advantage of online networking possibilities such as food stylist Web sites (see "Further Resources," below). Here you can post your work and begin to garner contacts within the industry.

Essential Gear

For veggie sweat, break out glycerin. Those are not beads of moisture on the tomatoes. They are drops of glycerin. A glycerin/water mixture, sometimes applied drop-by-drop, also makes the "sweat" on a cold glass. Veggies might also be just blanched to bring out their color, rather than completely cooked.

The U.S. Department of Labor does not keep track of food stylists, and, like many self-employed people in the culinary world, most food stylists slip between this job description and other related fields, such as chef and photographer. Therefore, getting an exact idea of how many people are working in this field, or their salaries, is difficult. A comparison with professional photographers may be useful. According to the U.S. Bureau of Labor Statistics, there were some 122,000 photographers employed in the United States in 2006. (Of course, only some of these were commercial photographers, which means the population of food stylists should be far smaller.) The median annual salary for salaried photographers was $26,170 in 2006, with the middle 50 percent earning between $18,680 and $38,730. The bottom 10 percent of photographers earned less than $15,540, while the highest-paid 10 percent earned upward of $56,640. Plainly, for many people, becoming a food stylist is either a part-time job or one skill among many; full-time food stylists are rare.

You Are Here

Take stock of your own resources before starting down the path to becoming a food stylist.

Do you have a background in food? In this case, you are in an excellent position to become a food stylist. You know how to mix ingredients, how things should look, and how to prepare appealing dishes. The chemistry and alchemy of the kitchen are no mystery to you. The problem is that in food styling, you do things to food that you would never do to things you would eat! The trick is learning how to make food look appealing to the camera instead of the human eye. There are many ways to do this. One is to pair with a photographer friend and experiment. Another is to apprentice as an assistant to an established food stylist. Before long, you will have your own portfolio and be able to take on clients of your own.

Navigating the Terrain

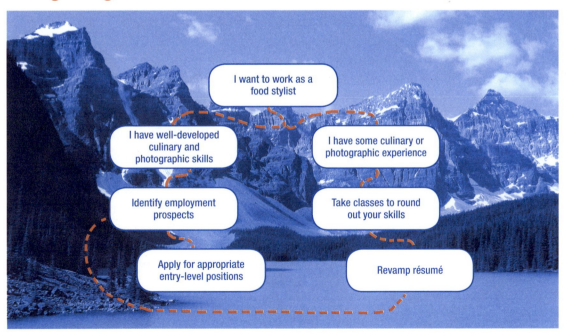

I want to work as a food stylist

I have well-developed culinary and photographic skills

I have some culinary or photographic experience

Identify employment prospects

Take classes to round out your skills

Apply for appropriate entry-level positions

Revamp résumé

Notes from the Field

Jennifer Ophir
Private chef and food stylist
New York, New York

What were you doing before you decided to change careers?
Retail store design (interiors of branded shops within department stores)

Why did you change your career?
I was bored, there was no challenge, and I had reached as far as I could go.

How did you make the transition?
It was tough. I had eight months off before I decided to go to cooking school. Then it was a mixture of winging it and being very mindful that I was 35 and starting my career over from square one and that a lot

Do you have a background in photography? A photography background is, in some ways, even better than a culinary background. You are already familiar with the demands of photography, and you have developed your eye for textures, camera angles, and light. The trick now is to learn to apply your knowledge to food. One way to do this might be to take a course at a local cooking school. Also consider shadowing a food stylist. There are also books that can help you on your way to food-styling glory. Check out, for instance, Linda Bellingham and Jean Ann Bybee's very interesting (and wonderfully illustrated) *Food Styling for Photographers: A Guide to Creating Your Own Appetizing Art*. You can build your food-styling repertoire by taking on small jobs in which the food stylist and photographer are one. Also work on creating a photography portfolio, both of food and other subject matter, in your spare time.

Do you need to get stylin'? If you do not have a background in either food or photography, then you need to get cracking. Learning about both fields is a must for an aspiring food stylist. There may also be specific courses on the field at a culinary school near you. In fact, completing a culinary-arts program will make you more qualified for all sorts of work, and may open possibilities you have never even considered. The same is true of photography courses. Though both fields are very detailed *of adjustments were going to be necessary. I know it sounds cliché, but I realized I needed to take a risk in order to get rewarded. Sometimes jumping in with your eyes closed is the best way to go and then swim with the current and see wear it takes you.*

What are the keys to success in your new career?

I do not know at this point. I guess I'm successful but I'm still trying to figure it all out. The food industry is so varied and now with chefs as the new rock stars, food and more importantly good food, is at the forefront in today's culture. So many options are available. I wear many hats, including cooking instructor, food stylist, recipe developer, artisanal food tour guide. But I always respect the food. Putting out my best for people to enjoy is what drives me.

and may be somewhat daunting for the beginner, it is necessary to have more than just a layman's knowledge if you are going to start creating a food stylist's portfolio.

Organizing Your Expedition

Before you set out, know where you are going.

Decide on a destination. To become a food stylist, you need two main areas of proficiency: photography and cuisine. Also, be aware that some elementary science skill is a necessary component of the job. You will need to utilize chemicals and various chemical processes to create the illusion of steam, for instance, or enhance the coloration of different foods. For a relatively specific field, there are many layers of knowledge one must be able to call upon at any given time in order to successfully complete the shoot.

Scout the terrain. Look for how you might be able to compensate for your shortcomings. If you do not have culinary experience, look at cooking schools near you. Some of these might even offer specialized courses in food styling. If photography is what you lack, there are many continuing-education programs that offer courses. The next possible step, after educational credentials, is to find a food stylist to assist.

Find the path that's right for you. To build your clientele, you need to get the word out about your services. One way to do this is to have your own Web site. Look into creating one yourself, or bartering or trading with someone with Web design experience. Also use the Internet to network. List yourself on Web sites and blogs read by those seeking food stylists (some suggestions are below), giving links to your online portfolio. Alternately, you might want to work your contact list, or send mailings to advertising firms, restaurants, and menu-printing companies.

Essential Gear

Don't drink the water. Gets bubbly under hot studio lights. Food stylists use cheap vodka instead. And those ice cubes? They are made of Lucite. Other beverages might have water added, so that light can filter through.

Landmarks

If you are in your twenties . . . You are in a good place to take up food styling. You will have special advantages if you are already well-versed in photography and/or cuisine. Remember that you will likely have to be a low-paid assistant for quite some time. Take advantage of this: It is how you will learn the job and make the necessary contacts. Meanwhile, keep on perfecting your own art. Build your portfolio, and work on getting your own gigs and taking beautiful still-life photos of food just for fun.

If you are in your thirties or forties . . . The midcareer changer without experience in cuisine or photography may have to return to school to update their credentials before getting that all-important assistantship. If, however, you already have the skills, you may be able to transition smoothly. Remember that the same things that go for twenty-something career changers go for you: people like to see skill in photography, culinary chops, and a portfolio of beautiful shots of food (which may result in many half-eaten boxes of cereal in your cabinets and half-cooked roasts in your dog's bowl). Whereas some food stylists may prefer younger assistants, cast your net wide and be persistent. You may also want to start your own blog of the photos you take on your own; this will help to get your name and style out there.

If you are in your fifties . . . Food styling has changed a lot in the past 25 years, and it is a career that definitely slants younger. This, however, is not to say that senior career changers cannot take up the trade, especially if they have related experience. A special strength in your case is the list of contacts you have built up over your career. Use your network, build your portfolio, and reach out to local establishments such as restaurants, advertising agencies, or regional magazines who may be in need of your services. Also, do not be afraid of technology: look to the Web to get the word out about your food stylist abilities.

Essential Gear

Burn the roast. Sorry, it is going in the trash after the shoot. The outside might be crisped by a handheld torch, but the inside's still raw. Also, you probably would not want to eat the wood varnish it is glazed with, nor get it too close to the lit cigarette you are using to produce "steam."

If you are over sixty . . . Food styling can be an excellent second career, particularly for those with a long history in the creative arts. While you have the same disadvantages as a senior career changer does, you also have the same strengths—a long list of contacts and business experience. Remember that a food stylist's portfolio counts more than anything else. Build up your clientele, reach out to local businesses and print media outlets, and get that Web site running!

Further Resources

Still Life With A food styling blog. http://stilllifewith.com
International Conference on Food Styling and Photography A biannual industry conference. http://www.foodstylingandphotography.org
Food Stylist and Food Styling Directory Part of Foodportfolio.com. http://www.foodportfolio.com/food_stylists/index.html

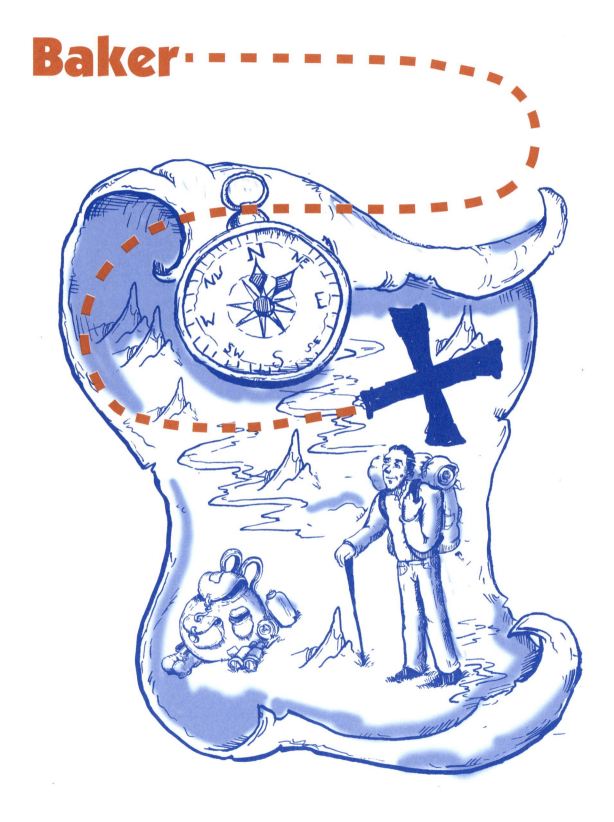

Baker

Baker

Career Compasses

Here's the breakdown of what it takes to become a baker.

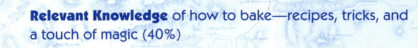

Relevant Knowledge of how to bake—recipes, tricks, and a touch of magic (40%)

Caring about what you are doing (20%)

Mathematical Skills since baking recipes are very by-the-numbers (20%)

Stress Management since things can get very hot in the kitchen (20%)

Destination: Baker

In many cultures, bread is so important that it is synonymous with "food." The first bread was probably created when Neolithic humans discovered that grinding and boiling grain into porridge made it more digestible. The next step was likely to bake this primitive dough into something resembling a tortilla or lavash. In time, it was discovered that allowing the dough to stand would make it rise thanks to the wild yeasts

Essential Gear

French bread culture. The stereotypical image of *les français* just would not be complete without a baguette held under-arm. In reality, the long, skinny baguette with its crispy crust is a relatively new way to consume bread. In the past, the French tended to eat bread in round loaves, but these are time-consuming to make, and a law passed in 1920 forbade bakers from working before 4 A.M. The baguette is less time-consuming to prepare, and thus became very popular. (It is also easier to take a bite off the end while you are walking home!) By law, the baguette must weigh 250 grams, and it classically contains nothing but flour, salt, water, and yeast. In fact, if bread contains anything else, French law requires it to be called by another name.

Because they do not contain preservatives, French baguettes tend to go stale very quickly. Of course, France also has *pain industriel* similar to what we eat here in the United States. The French word for crumb is "mie," giving us the term *pain de mie*, which is the French equivalent to familiar packaged white "loaf" bread (which is technically called a "Pullman loaf" in English). The bread is almost crustless because it is baked in a sealed pan. However, many French continue to buy their bread daily from the neighborhood *boulanger*. *Boulangeries* also sell pastries (such as croissants and *pain au chocolat*), cakes, tarts, and quiches, making them an excellent stop for a quick and inexpensive lunch while you are exploring Paris.

in the air, making the finished product even lighter and more digestible. The baking process also allows the human body to more fully access the nutrients in the grain. Thus did bread as we know it come to be.

At its simplest, bread contains nothing but flour, salt, water, and a leavening agent such as yeast, though it may also include milk, eggs, sugar, and seasonings, or other food items like cheese, fruit, vegetables, or nuts. The flour itself can be made from a variety of grains, such as wheat, corn, barley, rye, spelt, or millet. Flour is, of course, the most important ingredient. All flours share one thing in common: they are the milled endosperm of a grain. The proteins in the dough are what give it consistency. When water is added and the dough is kneaded, glutenin and gliadin dissolve to form gluten, a stringy structure of molecules. This develops further if the dough is allowed to "rest" and enzymes act on the gluten in a process called *autolysis*. Yeast digests the starches to produce gas bubbles, which may also be introduced to the dough by adding carbon dioxide or another element, such as baking soda, that produces gas. Bread varies by the type of leavening used. Sourdough, for instance, uses a special "starter" containing the necessary yeasts. This lightens the bread and changes the texture. The final step is to bake the bread. As everyone knows, the outer, crispy part is called the *crust*; however, fewer know that the mealy white part is called the *crumb* (as opposed to crumbs, which is what is left when you have finished).

All cultures have some version of bread, varying widely depending on agricultural conditions and traditional local food. In the Middle Ages, it was even used as part of the table setting, as food was served on "trenchers" of stale bread. It is a staple food, considered so important in Western culture that laws have been passed to regulate its size and consistency, and governments routinely act to stabilize its price. Medieval kings harshly punished short-changing bakers, the French Revolution began when bread prices rose too high because of poor crops, and French soldiers in the First World War were content to live on a daily ration of bread and wine. Even the Lord's Prayer asks, "give us this day our daily bread," and the beatniks of the 1950s introduced the slang term "bread" to mean "money."

Nonetheless, despite its deep cultural significance, bread has changed incredibly in the past century. Whereas in the past bread was created locally and consumed almost immediately, today, thanks to industrial agriculture, things are quite different. The uniform, pre-sliced loaves we see in the grocery store are the product of wheat that has been homogenized, uniformly milled in sterilized stainless-steel equipment, mixed in enormous vats to precise measurements, formed into identical loaves, baked in industrial ovens, and sliced identically. Because separating the bran out to make white bread also removes most of the nutritional content, nutrients are added, and because the loaves would otherwise go stale before reaching market, they are filled with preservatives. Other additives reduce mixing or fermenting time to speed up production. The resulting product is uniform in taste and appearance and ostensibly good for you, but bears little resemblance to what our ancestors would have recognized as "bread."

As people grow tired of these bland, mass-produced breads, and due to a burgeoning interest in European bread culture, artisanal bakers who make small batches of specialty breads have grown into a sizeable niche market. There is also an increasing awareness of the importance of whole grains in the diet, and a wish to avoid artificial ingredients, especially additives and preservatives, that many people feel are unhealthy. (Ironically, in the past, it was poorer people who ate coarser, whole-grain bread.) Of course, fresh, artisanal bread also simply *tastes* better—as anyone who has ever bought a fresh baguette from a French *boulangerie* knows full well.

Bakers may be specialized, creating one thing over and over (for instance, a bakery that supplies Italian bread to a city's restaurants), or they may produce small batches of many things. Other bakers produce specialty baked goods for small markets, such as gluten-free items for those living with celiac disease. Bakers who specialize in pastries are called *patissiers*. They often have specialized pastry degrees from culinary institutions. Some bakers work for themselves, owning their own bakeshops and pastry stores or even operating out of their homes, often supplying other businesses with their products. Some work for large companies, such as restaurants, supermarkets, caterers, specialty food stores, or institutions such as schools and hospitals. Bakers who work in industrial food-production facilities use high-volume mixing machines, enormous ovens, and ingredients measured by the sack. For our purposes, we will mainly concentrate on smaller-scale and artisanal baking as a career destination.

A good baker works well with others, has an eye for detail, and can follow instructions. There is a surprising amount of academic knowledge involved, too. Whether you are self-employed or working for someone else, a baking education is important. Bakers need to know not only just how to use their equipment, but also how to follow a recipe (or scale it up or down). You must know nutrition, sanitary laws, health and safety regulations, business skills such as budgeting, and the chemistry of how ingredients combine and are affected by heat and the production process. Pastry making is even more complicated: You must know how to make many different types of dough; what their properties are; the mechanical skills of how to mix, fold, and bake them; and how to make the finished result look attractive. A complicated project like a wedding cake is a masterpiece of design and planning.

One of the great things about becoming a baker is that it is a career that anyone can come from anywhere to do. All you need is a fine touch with an oven and a love of good bread. Your path is what you make it. You can start a home bakery to supply local coffee shops and restaurants, expanding it as your clientele grows; open your own pastry shop or bakery if you have enough capital; or look for employment with a larger company. There are no limits to what you can create—anything from bagels to baklava might fit into your niche. To enter into the field, bakers can go through a process of apprenticeship, or enroll in a baking program at a certified culinary institute or through a correspondence course. Certification is also available through the Retail Bakers of America, which offers four levels of certification and tests in areas that include sanitation, management, retail sales, and how to train a staff. To be certified as a master baker you must complete 60 hours of coursework (30 hours each in sanitation and professional development) and have eight years of experience.

According to the U.S. Bureau of Labor Statistics, there were 149,000 bakers employed all across the United States in 2006, and the demand for their services will only grow. The median annual earnings for a baker was $22,030 in May, 2006; the middle 50 percent made between $17,720 and $28,190, the top 10 percent made more than $35,380, and the bottom 10 percent made less than $15,180. The highest earnings in the industries that employed the largest amounts of bakers were a median of $22,580 (in bakeries and tortilla manufacturing) and $22,170 (in grocery stores). Needless to say, free baked goods are a perk of the job!

You Are Here

Take stock of your own resources before starting down the path to becoming a baker.

Do you have a background in food? In this case, you probably already have much of the knowledge you need to become a baker. You are familiar with food chemistry, sanitary practices, nutrition, and other necessary items. You may have even done some baking yourself. The next step is to decide on a plan, and, if you do not have it, get formal baking experience. With regard to the latter, consider a baking or pastry certificate from a culinary school. With regard to the former, decide if you want to become someone else's employee, or start your own business. (For more on starting your own business, see the appendix.)

Navigating the Terrain

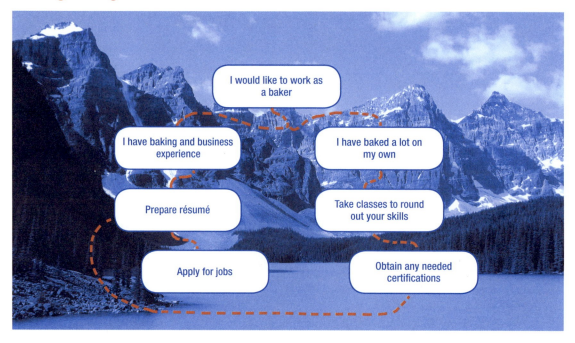

I would like to work as a baker

I have baking and business experience

I have baked a lot on my own

Prepare résumé

Take classes to round out your skills

Apply for jobs

Obtain any needed certifications

Do you have a background in business? Business experience can place a baker in good stead, especially if he or she intends to open his or her own bakery. As a business professional, you know all about budgeting, marketing, and having a business plan. You can think analytically and know how to balance income and expenses. The trick, then, is getting baking experience. Find a good culinary school, and enroll in their baking and pastry arts program.

Do you need to rise to the occasion? In this case, you are starting from scratch. You can learn by doing—but an even better plan is to get the education you need. Besides taking baking and pastry courses at a culinary school, look to also take some classes in business. Of course, you can always try to find a job working for someone else—and more than likely, the experience will do you good—but you will also want to keep your options open. In fact, if you have never worked in the food world before, it is a good idea to consider getting a job as a baker's assistant or apprentice. This is a good way to learn the ropes.

Notes from the Field

Sonya Matos
Baker
New York, New York

What were you doing before you decided to become a baker?

I wore many linked hats. I was a partner at an applications training firm while temping as an EDGAR [a professional services reporting program] operator, legal word processor and help desk analyst.

Why did you become a baker?

My partnership dissolved and I did not like what was being offered to me in the legal support field. My husband suggested the cookies and since we live an organic lifestyle, I insisted on clean food. I make great baked goods that everyone demands every holiday. By the way, this is my third career shift—from secretary/student to scientist to word processor/legal word processor trainer/help desk analyst to baker (which is very scientific in nature. You could say I've come back to science.) I actually worked my way through college as an administrative assistant.

How did you make the transition?

I'm still transitioning. I took the money from the reimbursement from the last business and financed this one. I used my usual recipes but had to adjust the recipes for organic ingredients.

What are the keys to success as a baker?

I'm still too new to this to call it a success at this time. I just started the business in May and am involved in setting up a proper corporate structure and business plan. I am searching for organic farmers' markets in the tri-state area to form my "bread and butter" base for the business.

Organizing Your Expedition

Before you set out, know where you are going.

Decide on a destination. To become a baker, you obviously need to know how to bake. But there is a lot more to it than that. Decide what you want to specialize in: Pastry? Bread? Specialty goods? Furthermore, where do you see yourself: With your own bakery? Working for some-one else? All of this will guide what steps you take in your culinary education.

Scout the terrain. Research cooking programs in your area. Amongst the questions you need to ask are what certification they have, how far they are from your home and present place of work, how long a course will take, and how much it will cost. Are evening programs available if you want to keep working while going to school? How will you finance your education? The school can usually help you research financial aid solutions. Decide also what level of education you are seeking, whether a simple certificate or a four-year degree. Do they offer work experience and internship placement? All of these are important factors in your training.

Find the path that's right for you. The two paths you can head down as a baker are working for someone else or starting your own business. The first is fairly straightforward: Get the necessary education and expe-rience, look around for opportunities, and apply for jobs. If you are open-ing your own business, you need to do some additional planning. One of the most important things is to size up and address your target market. What opportunities exist in your area? Do you see yourself making arti-san breads for gourmands? Gluten-free products? Muffins and scones for local coffeehouses? Where will you sell it? Through your own store? At local farmer's markets? Over the Internet?

Landmarks

If you are in your twenties . . . Twenty-somethings are in an excellent position to change their careers and become bakers. Whether you are working in the culinary field or not, this is a good time of life to devote to exploration, training, and going back to school. While you may not be put in charge of a whole baking operation overnight, and you might not have access to the capital you would need to start your own business, everyone has to begin somewhere. Build up your business experience, and look for internships, apprenticeships, and entry-level jobs that will teach you even more and help you get ahead.

If you are in your thirties or forties . . . The culinary arts, and baking in general, are a popular destination for midcareer changers. In many ways, baking is less demanding and has more regular hours than many other food-related occupations, such as catering and being a restaurant chef. Baking is also a good place to turn to if you have been out of the workforce for a while, since it is easy to start and grow a home business. But there is no need to set your sights low: The future is as wide-open as you choose to make it.

If you are in your fifties . . . Why not take your years of experience and put them to work for you? Senior career changers often have a wealth of business experience and capital at their disposal. What is more, they are well attuned to their communities, and know what their neighbors' needs are—whether it is vegan carrot muffins or gluten-free brownies. Whether you choose to work out of your home, supply your community with French-style baguettes from your own storefront, or seek a job working at someone else's bakery, make your long work history work for you.

If you are over sixty . . . One of the great things about baking is that you can do it at any age! You may not want to spend your golden years running a shop, but why not start your own small business selling baked goods made at home? Of course, all of the baking ideas suggested for younger career changers are open to you, too. Seek out farmer's markets and other agricultural fairs and festivals to sell your products, as well. There is no reason why "Nana's Bakery" cannot become the next big food trend to hit your area!

Further Resources

Retail Bakers of America Offering industry advocacy and certification. http://www.rbanet.com
The American Culinary Association The trade organization for professional chefs and Bakers; also certifies culinary schools. http://www.acfchefs.org

Bartender

Bartender

Career Compasses

Here's the breakdown of what it takes to become a bartender.

Relevant Knowledge of drink recipes, brands of liquor, mixology, and specialty beers (40%)

Caring about your customers—a bartender is often an impromptu shoulder to cry on (30%)

Mathematical Skills since you will have to calculate tabs and make change on the fly (10%)

Stress Management since everyone wants your attention (20%)

Destination: Bartender

While some jobs might be more lucrative, more glamorous, or more high-powered than bartending, few seem to offer the sheer amount of fun. What could be cooler than being paid to work where so many people choose to hang out? As the bartender, you can see yourself as the life of the party, making conversation and socializing with customers. After all, everyone loves the bartender, do they not? And it is not like a real job, right? In reality, bartending is hard, stressful work. The hours are long and irregular, the pay can be bad, and the job requires you to constantly

53

Essential Gear

Cocktail recipes. The term "cocktail" first shows up in the turn of the 19th century as "a stimulating liquor composed of spirits of any kind, sugar, water, and bitters." Sources differ as to the etymology, whether it was the "tail" of the dregs of liquor left in the stop-cock of the barrel, or a drink mixed with the tail feathers of an actual cock. No matter what the source, here are some recipes to get you started.

Martini. Properly, vermouth (dry white or sweet red) and gin in an approximately 5:1 ratio, though duels have been fought over the proper way to prepare this. Some people like more gin for a "drier" martini. Winston Churchill used gin that had "looked at a vermouth bottle across the room."

Mojito. A traditional Cuban drink made popular by Cuban immigrants in Miami. It contains white rum, sugar (or, better, sugar cane juice), lime, soda water, and mint. One adds the lime juice to the sugar or syrup and mint leaves, which are gently mashed to release the mint oils. Rum is added, then ice and soda water. Make sure to pick the mint out of your teeth afterward.

Margarita. The power of tequila, mellowed with an orange liqueur such as triple sec and lime juice, often either blended with or served over ice, and salt on the rim. The tequila/liqueur/juice ratios vary widely, however 2:1:1, 3:2:1, and1:1:1 are the most common ratios. The International Bartender's Association's guide demands a ratio of 7:4:3. A fun activity to do at home is to see what mix is your favorite. Such an experiment can easily occupy an entire weekend.

Long Island Iced Tea. Long Island iced tea contains no actual tea, though it might contain ice. What it does contain is a great deal of liquor: vodka, gin, tequila, and rum, sometimes with triple sec, sour mix, and cola.

Suffering Bastard. The Suffering Bastard originated because Trader Vic's sold it in tiki mugs that looked as if they were suffering from bad hangovers. It contains equal parts gin, rum, and ginger ale, half a portion of lime juice, a dash of bitters, and ice.

divide your attention. You may have to know hundreds or even thousands of drink recipes, keep track of whose tab is where, and deal with drunk or belligerent customers. There is also a lot of not-so-fun work to do: lifting heavy kegs of beer, taking inventory, and cleaning glassware.

The job of a bartender (or barkeep, barmaid, tapster, or mixologist) is, quite simply, to serve beverages from behind a bar. You must know how to mix many drinks, from a simple gin and tonic to more elaborate mojitos, artful martinis, and far-out drinks like a Corpse Reviver. You will need to know how to pour a pint of Guinness (it takes practice). You will need to take money from customers and servers, make correct change, and keep track of tabs. If the bar does not have a bouncer stationed at the door to check IDs, you need to make sure that customers are of legal drinking age and decide when someone has had too much to drink. You may also hand out promotional materials for beer and liquor brands, deal with distributors, take deliveries of stock, and, in some jurisdictions, sell cigarettes. Though many larger establishments use automatic equipment that measures and mixes drinks with the mere push of a button, you may need to work quickly to keep up with the flood of drink requests.

As the bartender, you are the "public face" of the drinking establishment. Bar owners often hire bartenders whose "look" meshes well with the bar's identity: regular-guy for a place where corporate salarymen unwind, model-attractive for a hot nightspot or trendy bar, mature for a "traditional" establishment, tattooed with long hair for a biker bar or punk club. You may be called upon to answer questions ranging from sports scores to the location of a good Thai restaurant in the neighborhood. It is helpful to be a good listener. In seriousness or not, you will be called upon to act as a sympathetic ear and impromptu personal counselor.

Bartenders tend to work for other people. The term *barkeep* generally denotes an owner-bartender. (Opening your own bar, however, could be the subject of a whole book in itself. Besides the thousand-and-one choices you have to make in theme, product, and atmosphere, there are a plethora of local, state, and federal regulations regarding the sale of alcohol.) Bartending is a popular profession. According to the U.S Bureau of Labor Statistics, there were 495,000 bartenders working in America as of 2006, and the number is expected to grow to 551,000 by 2016. (In Montana, fully one percent of the workforce bartended in 2004!) Bartenders made median hourly earnings of $7.86 in 2006, with the middle 50 percent earning between $6.77 and $10.10, the lowest 10 percent earning less than $6.00/hour, and the highest 10 percent earning more than $13.56 per hour. Of course these statistics do not include tips, often the largest part of the bartender's income. Note also that these statistics are not the same throughout the United States: Bartenders who work in wealthier areas or more expensive establishments tend to make more.

Becoming a bartender is relatively easy. Unfortunately, the prime requisite (as with many other culinary careers) is prior experience. How to get around this catch-22? Well, a Google search for "bartending school" brings up about 550,000 results—one for every bartender in the country! Courses may last from one evening to several weeks, and cost anywhere from a pittance to thousands of dollars. Some bartending schools even have job-placement programs. The problem is that a lot of bar owners are not impressed by the credential. If they see a bartending school on your résumé, they will likely turn to another applicant who has more hands-on experience. Simply knowing the ingredients of hundreds of drinks does not mean that you can make one under the stress of a late-night rush. The more secure way to become a bartender is to start as a server, barback, or by making drinks at catering events or other such places. This is hard, demanding work, but it is invaluable experience. Watch the bartenders and learn what is in various drinks. Ask questions. See how the bartenders interact with their customers. A bartending school can give you the finishing touches, but it is not how you learn to bartend.

Finally, two things to bear in mind. First, the truth is that the attractive and the outgoing have a definite advantage in the bartending profession for a reason. Bars are businesses, and like all businesses, they exist for one purpose: to move product. The reason why people come to your bar is because it is cooler, more home-like, or has better buffalo wings than the other places on the block. Your job is to keep them coming back and to sell drinks, no matter what it takes—remembering names, favorite drinks, and personal woes. Your tip is your commission on the sale. Why do so many actors and models work in bars while they are waiting for their breaks? The answer is because they are good at dealing with people and showing the face that they want to show to the to world. Second, be aware that bartending is a bad job choice for those with a propensity to drink too much. Not only is being around all that alcohol a temptation, but the more you drink, the less effective you are behind the bar, and the more you drink up the profits. Bartenders who drink too much quickly find themselves without jobs. Accordingly, a good bartender has a warm, open, outgoing personality, but is not *too* much of a party person. The job requires a measure of discipline as well as fun.

You Are Here

See what is on tap before starting down the path to becoming a bartender.

Do you have a background in food or sales? This is a helpful beginning. You are used to recipes and handling point-of-sale interactions—but that is not everything. The best way to get hired as a bartender is proven experience, and the only way to get experience is by working alongside other bartenders. Look for jobs as a barback in bars or pubs, pay close attention to the bartender, and work your way up. One hint is that restaurants tend to be less picky about who tends the bar. If you have experience working in the food service industry and know how to make a decent number of drinks, they are more likely to give you a try.

Navigating the Terrain

I want to become a bartender

Get an entry-level job

Look into attending bartending school

Build experience

Find a job

Notes from the Field

Molly Prunka
Bartender
New York, New York

What were you doing before you decided to change careers?

I graduated from Fordham University in 2007 with a degree in marketing and international economics. Before bartending, I worked at various advertising agencies and the PR department of the Walt Disney Company.

Why did you change your career?

I became a bartender to make a lot of money, fast. I moved to the East Village after graduating and found a sports bar called Village Pourhouse that was hiring. I applied, waitressed, and worked up to bartending. I love it.

How did you make the transition?

The transition was easy. I took a year off before going to advertising portfolio design school at the Miami Ad School in San Francisco to

Are you a people person? If you are coming in from acting, modeling, being a sales rep, or another people-oriented profession, you are ahead of the game. Bartending is in a similar vein. But again, this is not everything. You need the necessary technical experience to go with your people skills. Consider working as a drinks server for nightclubs or other brand promotions. Though they are often one-time gigs, they will give you a chance to interact with other bartenders and perhaps learn a few tricks of the trade, as well as provide necessary résumé-building experience.

Got to mix it up a bit? No problem! In fact, you are not as far behind as you may think. Look for that all-important entry-level job as a barback or server. Emphasize any previous experience you may have had in the food-service business. Also remember that while attending a bartending school can help, it no guaranteed shortcut to gaining a position.

become an art director. It was a breath of fresh air from working at agencies.

I wear ripped jeans, a tank top and I can be as pleasant as I feel like that day. It's like no other job in the world. I recommend everyone work in bar service at some point. What are the keys to success in your new career?

The keys to being a successful bartender are reading customers and being fast. Some people want you to be polite, others almost want you to insult them. You make tips from interacting, and from serving quickly. If it is too busy to play with your customers, get drinks in hands as fast as possible. Run, think ahead, keep busy. Do that faster than another bartender and you have won repeat clients.

Work well with your coworkers! Enjoy them! They are here to make money too, so do not get greedy. Do not ever argue about money with a coworker, just give in. Working for no creative outlet, or no end result besides monetary gain is stressful and disheartening. Do not let it ruin you.

Organizing Your Expedition

Before you set out, know where you are going.

Decide on a destination. Before you begin your search, figure out exactly what sort of bartending you want to do. Do you want to work at a hip nightspot? On cruise ships? For a catering company? Do you have a dream of opening your own Irish pub? Each of these goals necessitates a different plan, but no matter where you enter into the field you can only work your way up through experience. Talk to people at the venues in which you are interested in working and see what specific credentials will set you above the rest. Remember that most bartending schools do not have accreditation, and many of their courses are not worth the large amounts of money they charge.

Scout the terrain. Look for entry-level jobs in the sorts of places you might like to work. In most venues, this will mean working as a *barback*, or bartender's assistant. Barbacks clean glassware, keep the bartender well supplied with beer, liquor, garnishes, ingredients, and ice, and might also make simple drinks and pour wine and beer. You might also be able to pick up regular bartending shifts at less-busy times or covering for one of the usual bartenders. Restaurants tend to give you more leeway in this. If you have ample food-service experience, you are more likely to get a shot behind the bar.

Find the path that's right for you. If you do well as a barback, you will be given more and more responsibility. Parlay this into regular bartending gigs. Many up-and-coming bartenders might work as a barback as a steady job at one venue, while picking up regular shifts at another. The main thing is that the owner must trust you to do a good job. Once you have the skills, you can take them anywhere. Note that it may be necessary to bartend in a locale you *do not* want to work in (i.e., a restaurant) before you get hired in a place where you *do* want to work (i.e., that trendy club). Do not knock working your way up the ladder—it is the only way to the top.

Landmarks

If you are in your twenties . . . The bar scene thrives on twenty-somethings. Your first step should be to find a good barback job. Ask around at your local watering holes if they know of anyone in need of help. Professional bar-staff talk to each other an awful lot, which means that they will know all the latest news and potential job leads. But be warned: this goes both ways. If you do not perform well at the job, word will travel.

If you are in your thirties or forties . . . The procedure for working your way into the bartending world is the same at any age. If you can find (and afford) a reputable bartending school that has job placement, this may help you, but if not, be prepared to work entry-level jobs for a while. Make sure that you are a good fit with the place you are looking to work—which may mean shedding some of the vestiges of the business world you have left behind. Also look into nontraditional bartending gigs with catering companies, on cruise ships, or other such places. You might also want to use your personal beverage-related interests (are you a microbrew fanatic? an oenophile?) to help you secure employment.

If you are in your fifties . . . Though older career changers may balk at the required apprenticing process for becoming a bartender, they also have advantages that younger career changers do not. One is a social network that may include bar owners. Ask them to show you the ropes. Another possibility is opening your own place, or buying into an establishment with partners and fellow-investors. If money is not an object and you have always dreamed of having your own British-style pub, this may be the best route to take.

If you are over sixty . . . All of the things that apply to senior career changers apply to you. Also remember that people of all ages drink. What is to stop you from opening a bar in your neighborhood? You may not be at the age where you can lug kegs of beer, but there is no maximum age to tend bar. Look for the opportunities all around you, and take advantage of them!

Further Resources

The International Bartenders Association Representing (and recognizing) the best bartenders in the world. http://iba-world.net/english/index.php

Bartender's Database A wiki-style compendium of useful information. http://www.bartendersdatabase.com/index.php?title=main_page

Food Service Manager

Food Service Manager

Career Compasses

Here's the breakdown of what it takes to become a food service manager.

Relevant Knowledge of how the food service business works (25%)

Caring about doing a good job and that your customers are happy (25%)

Organizational Skills since the job is all about keeping things organized (25%)

Stress Management is necessary to multi-task and keep everything running (25%)

Destination: Food Service Manager

Food service management is organizing and directing the daily activity of restaurants, catering halls, cafeterias, and other places where food is served. Obviously, this is a huge and complicated job description, and no two food service manager's experiences are exactly alike. A food service manager might be a restaurant owner (about 45 percent, according to the U.S. Bureau of Labor Statistics), a general or assistant manager, or even an executive chef who has gone from the kitchen to running a significant proportion of the business end of the enterprise. Because the job

Essential Gear

A brief history of the restaurant. Restaurants in one form or another are probably as old as civilization. Whereas nomadic peoples such as the Bedouins are famous for their hospitality to travelers, the facts of city life, such as scarcities of time and resources, open up ample niches for professional food-preparers. Roman cities had establishments to serve snacks to busy travelers and meals to the poor, who did not have kitchens in their apartments. The oldest documented restaurant is the Sobrino de Botin in Madrid, which opened in 1725, but the Stiftskeller St. Peter in Salzburg claims to have been started in 803 under the reign of Emperor Charlemagne.

The term "restaurant" itself dates to pre-Revolutionary France. Originally referring to a hearty ("restoring") soup, the term was applied to a dining establishment as early as 1765. However, the majority of high-class entertaining took place in private homes, as aristocrats vied with one another to set the best, most inventive, and most lavish table. It was only after the French Revolution that European *haute cuisine* moved out of the kitchens and into public spaces. Left unemployed by the aristocrats who fled the country, private chefs found a niche cooking first for the masses of provincials who flocked to the capital, and then for the new aristocracy that came in after Napoleon's rise. Where France led the rest of the world followed. The first restaurant in America, "Jullien's Restarator," opened in Boston in 1794. Interestingly, at this point, food was served *service á la française*, or what we would call "family style." The later development where waiters would bring out courses is called *service á la russe*.

description is pretty much the same whether or not you are the owner (a large part of the difference is whether you draw a salary or live off the profits), we will consider both restaurant owners and professional managers together simply as food service managers. (For more on starting your own business, see our appendix on the subject.)

Generally speaking, a food service manager has to coordinate between various teams, such as the kitchen and the waitstaff, make sure things are set up and broken down properly, ensure hygiene and health and safety, and see to customer satisfaction. Other parts of the job include making sure the physical equipment (refrigerators, stoves, pots and pans, as well as the facilities such as the dining room, table and chairs, and bathrooms) are clean and in good repair, ordering new equipment if necessary, and making sure that dangerous situations do not arise. Food service managers take stock of inventory and order new supplies—not just food, but such things as napkins, tablecloths, soap and floor cleaner—as needed.

Food service managers are also in charge of human resources. This means that they recruit, train, and sometimes have to fire employees. Recruiting is often done through career fairs, visits to culinary schools, or advertisements placed in the newspaper or on the Internet. Training might be as simple as showing the new dishwasher how to operate the pressure washer, or it might mean assigning a trainee chef to an experienced mentor. Once employees have been trained, food service managers must try to retain them, which is a constant challenge in the high-turnover world of food service. Creating and arranging schedules is another duty; in the case of absences, food service managers have to "float" to do whatever job needs to be done—from taking out the garbage to waiting tables to cooking dinner. Food service managers might also handle human resources-related administrative tasks such as government forms, worker's eligibility, worker's compensation claims, audits and the like. This usually includes taking care of taxes by withholding for Social Security and unemployment, distributing the payroll, keeping track of everyone's hours, pooling tips, and paying and monitoring suppliers' invoices.

Added to this are the financial responsibilities. Food service managers make sure that the day's receipts are reconciled with the cash the restaurant has taken in. They deal with credit card companies. They may need to take the day's earnings to the bank or lock them up in a safe, which can be a hazardous job since it leaves you vulnerable to robbery. Finally, at the end of the night's work, no matter how tired the manager is, he or she may have to lock up, make sure the ovens, grills, and lights are off, and the burglar alarm is on. If there is an emergency in the middle of the night, the food service manager is often the one to respond. If you are the owner, you will also need to make strategic business decisions, such as budgeting. How will you pay the rent? Do you buy a new refrigerator, or a new gas grill? Sometimes the decisions hit close to home: Do you buy a new car, or reinvest the profits in the restaurant?

Customer satisfaction is one of the trickiest parts of the food service manager's job description. You have to make sure that everything is on schedule so that customers are served in a timely fashion. If there are backups in the kitchen, the manager may have to work with the chef and the rest of the kitchen staff to clear the jam. They also oversee the seating of customers and the timely clearing of tables. If there are problems or complaints, the food service manager must deal with them. On the other hand, a warm, welcoming manager who takes personal interest in each and every guest helps to add a "family" feel to the restaurant and turns the occasional diner into a regular.

A food service manager has a long, varied workday. You are usually the first to arrive when the restaurant opens and the last to leave. This means you may work 12 to 15 hours a day, seven days a week. However, if you are lucky enough to work in an institution such as a school or hospital, you may have more regular hours since you are running a more standardized, bureaucratic establishment with normal opening and closing times, perhaps dividing the responsibility with other people who share your job description. No matter where you work, you will probably be on your feet a lot, and exposed to the minor cuts, burns, pulled muscles, and other aches and pains that all food service workers suffer.

For all of their work, however, food service managers can make a decent amount of money. The 65 percent of food service managers who were salaried brought home median annual earnings of $43,020 in 2006, with the middle 50 percent earning between $34,210 and $55,100, the

Navigating the Terrain

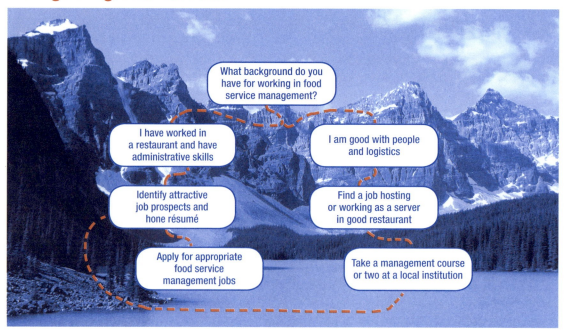

What background do you have for working in food service management?

I have worked in a restaurant and have administrative skills

I am good with people and logistics

Identify attractive job prospects and hone résumé

Find a job hosting or working as a server in good restaurant

Apply for appropriate food service management jobs

Take a management course or two at a local institution

lowest 10 percent making less than $27,400 and the highest 10 percent more than $70,810. Those who worked at full-service restaurants made a median annual salary of $45,650. There were about 350,000 people working as food service managers in the United States in 2006, according to the U.S Bureau of Labor Statistics, and their numbers are expected to grow more slowly than average, to about 368,000 in 2016.

There are no formal education requirements to becoming a food service manager. Being able to do the job, perhaps working your way up from elsewhere in the restaurant world, is qualification enough. Being calm and able to handle pressure and multitask are also essential qualities. Nonetheless, there are programs offered in food service management. Some of these are certification programs, others are full two- or four-year degrees. In fact, almost 1,000 colleges or universities in the United States offer four-year degrees in restaurant and hospitality management or institutional food service management. Opinions vary on whether these programs help you get a job; some employers prefer to see such a program on your résumé, but overall it is experience that is most important.

Formal training aside, there are many useful—even essential—skills that a food service manager needs. Knowledge of Spanish is helpful, since many kitchen staff and restaurant workers may only speak English as a second language. Some municipalities require that food service managers have certain certifications, such as food sanitation. Being good with computers is essential, since many restaurant use computers (called "POS," or point-of-sale systems) to keep track of inventory, sales, and employee hours. Besides the POS system, you may need Internet skills, not just to recruit employees, but perhaps also to build and maintain a Web site for your restaurant or to monitor industry news and see what people are saying about your establishment.

You Are Here

How to manage becoming a food service manager? Ask yourself these basic questions.

Do you have a background in food service? This is an excellent background for someone who wants to become a food service manager. You already know how the business is run, and you have experience with all the concerns that come up in the normal course of doing things. It is for

Notes from the Field
Jason Spears
Restaurant owner/manager
New York, New York

What were you doing before you decided to change careers?

I was a mechanical engineer working as a process engineer and product designer.

Why did you change your career?

I always knew I wanted to open a restaurant or café. I had fully developed concepts in my head years before I ever did anything about it. It is not that I disliked engineering; I wanted to make my ideas real. And most of all, everything happened when it was time for it to happen; you have to be in the perfect place in your life, with the right people around you, with the right finances, with the ability to leave your job or work on your business on the side. Everything has to line up right, and it did for me.

How did you make the transition?

First, there was a distinct switch in mindset. I became 100 percent focused on and driven to start my business. Then, an insane amount of work. My planning started in my free time (every second I had free). Then, as it began to form, I started spending my free time plus most of my work day (secretly) working on opening my restaurant. Once I knew it was real, I started telling everyone I knew what I was doing, for support, marketing, and money. I opened my first place when I was still working as an engineer. I was lucky enough to have a partner who

this reason that most food service managers are promoted from within the ranks. Nonetheless, it might strengthen your case to have some formal academic experience. Look for courses or even certificate or degree programs in your area.

Do you have a background in management? While food service management has its own particular challenges, it is not too different from other sorts of management. Prior business experience is also useful when opening your own restaurant: budgets, calculating profits and loss, and long-term planning are not particular to any industry. Nonetheless, *picked up the day shift, and I would go straight from work to my café, where I worked late. Got up the next morning and did it again. Once cash flow could pay my salary, I became a full time business owner.*

What are the keys to success in your new career?

It is truly never-ending work. You have to be willing to work 18 hour days, seven days a week, at least for the first couple of years until you have developed processes and management that allow you to be away. And even then, the most successful restaurants have very hands-on owners. So it follows that in order to work that much, you better love your job. Secondly, you need to be well funded. Do not consider the best case when determining the capital required. Consider the worst case. If you cannot raise that, do not try. This is the most commonly ignored advice, and the most common cause of the failure of restaurants. If you are a good operator, you can succeed with the right amount of money. But even the best operator can lose, and lose big, for a while. So be ready for that. Finally, you need to genuinely know your business. The personality and background of the owner shines through to the dining room and service, like it or not. If you want to open a Peruvian cuisine restaurant you better be from Peru, or have lived there for a long time; otherwise your customers will see right through you. Do not try to fake it. The most likely restaurants to succeed are genuine. Also, you need to know the restaurant business. It is not as simple as cooking at home. You need to really understand commercial cooking, accounting, management, marketing, construction, human resources, customer service, bartending.

there is a steep learning curve for food service-specific items. If you feel like you are not quite ready for the challenge, or just want to know what you will be facing, consider taking courses in food service, hospitality, or restaurant management. These are available as night or extension courses through many universities. Volunteer work is also another great way of getting experience.

Are you coming into this from nowhere? Whether you have always dreamed of owning your own restaurant or want to work for a national chain, you will need to learn the business from the bottom up. This means finding an entry-level post in restaurant management, such as assistant manager. If nothing of the sort is available, enter into the field in any capacity: as a waiter or waitress, bartender, or host or hostess. A food service manager must be able to do all these tasks indiscriminately, from bussing tables to waiting on customers to working in the kitchen.

Organizing Your Expedition

Before you set out, know where you are going.

Decide on a destination. What, exactly, do you want to do in food service management? Do you see yourself owning your own restaurant? Managing a national chain? Working as the manager for an establishment you already know? Your final goals will dictate what path you take. National corporate chains generally have an established set of criteria that they look for. Research what these are, whether it is work experience, academic certificates, or both, and work toward this goal. If, on the other hand, you want to work for yourself, the prime requisite is being able to walk the walk. Practical experience is the best teacher in this case.

Scout the terrain. Look for job opportunities near you. Perhaps someone in your social network is a restaurant owner, and can spot you a few shifts so you can get oriented, or perhaps there are volunteer positions at a local soup kitchen, senior feeding program, or not-for-profit. Also research culinary schools, colleges, and universities in your area. Do they have courses that meet your needs and goals? What exactly are you looking for—an extension course, a certificate, an associate's degree, or a four-year degree? Will you go to school part-time or full-time? Finally, research legalities in your area. Will you need to have certification in sanitation or food safety, for instance? If you are going to start your own restaurant, look for a business mentor (see the appendix for more details).

Find the path that's right for you. Once you have worked out what you need to do, the trick is making it happen. One big concern is money. How will you finance your education or the start-up costs of your restaurant?

How will you pay your rent or mortgage while you are taking entry-level positions? Each person's path to food service management will be different. Some may have friends in the business willing to give them a chance; others will have to jump through a series of hoops. Persistence is the key.

Landmarks

If you are in your twenties . . . This is a good time of life to start training for a food service management position. While you may not have the required capital or experience, remember that this is a long-term goal. In the meanwhile, work your way up in the food service world. Learn as many jobs as you can and volunteer to gain additional responsibility. Earning trust is difficult, but worth it. Meanwhile, look into taking résumé-enhancing courses in food service management.

If you are in your thirties or forties . . . Midcareer changers have the advantages of maturity and a proven ability to handle responsibility, both seen as essential in candidates for management positions. Nonetheless, you will still need a proven track record of food service, or at least management experience. While your previous experience counts for something, you may also want to take food-service specific courses. This is also the time in life when you may have built up enough capital and credit to start your own restaurant.

If you are in your fifties . . . The challenges that apply to midcareer changers also apply to senior career changers. Again, be careful if you start your own business. Know what you are getting into. Opening a restaurant is not a respite from the problems of the workaday corporate world; if anything, it is a whole new set of challenges.

If you are over sixty . . . There is absolutely nothing stopping a second-career starter from becoming a food service manager. The food service industry has no mandatory retirement age; if anything, the cap is the enormous amount of energy that the job requires. Still, if you feel you have what it takes to become a food service manager, and have the knowledge and experience it takes to back it up, then go for it! Be sure to stress past leadership experience, organizational skills, and the ability to multitask in your conversations with potential employers.

Further Resources

National Restaurant Association Professional development and industry advocacy for the restaurant industry. Includes a job bank. http://www.restaurant.org

National Restaurant Association Educational Foundation The NRA's educational arm. Essential resources for becoming a food service manager. http://www.nraef.org

Council on Hotel, Restaurant, and Institutional Education A professional organization for those engaged in educating tomorrow's managers in the hospitality and tourism industries. http://www.chrie.org

Brewer or Winemaker

Brewer or Winemaker

Career Compasses

Here's the breakdown of what it takes to become a brewer or winemaker.

Relevant Knowledge of brewing or winemaking, which includes a refined palate (60%)

Caring about fine beer and wine (20%)

Mathematical Skills to calculate ratios, modify recipes, etc. (10%)

Organizational Skills to track numerous ongoing process (10%)

Destination: Brewer or Winemaker

Brewers are the alchemists who turn water, barley, and hops (and sometimes other ingredients) into the liquid gold known as beer. Winemakers (properly called *vintners*) transform grapes into wine. Brewing and winemaking are two of the world's oldest professions. The first beer probably came about when Neolithic humans left their porridge out overnight and discovered that the resulting liquid was not only tasty and good for you, but also made you feel good. Wine probably resulted from the same discovery with grape juice. No matter what their origins, though, beer and wine are as old as human civilization. Evidence for beer production dates back to ancient Egypt and Mesopotamia, and the first known recipe is a Sumerian formula for beer.

Today, brewing and winemaking are multi-billion dollar industries. According to the Census bureau, there were 347 breweries in the United States in 2002 (the last year for which data is available). They employed 28,000 people, had total payrolls of almost $1.5 billion, and made almost $11 billion in profits. Over 230 of these breweries had four or fewer employees. In addition, there were 1,420 "craft breweries" operating in the United States in 2007, according to the industry Web site beertown.org. *Craft brewery* is an industry term for beer that is brewed without adjuncts (unmalted grains) and with an eye to "style." Generally, it refers to small-batch, high quality beer as opposed to the popular mass-market styles put out by the large breweries.

Wine is a similarly massive industry, employing around 1 million people with a total payroll of around $33 billion. Grapes were the highest-valued American food crop in 2006, at around $3.3 billion—two-thirds of which was grown for juice and winemaking. From June 2005 to July 2006, over 780 million gallons of wine were made in the United States, with a value of $23.8 billion. About 90 percent of it was made in California, though wineries can be found in every state. Though America is only 38th in per-capita wine consumption worldwide (up from 60th a few years ago), the industry is growing at a rapid pace. Much as with craft brewing, there are many small, high-quality wineries. Most of them produce less than 5,000 cases per year, accounting for about 2 percent of wine sales.

Though the microbrewing and craft vinting revolution seems rather modern, in reality it is a return to the way things were in the past. The newfound legality of home brewing the United States in 1978 (wine has been legal to make at home since the repeal of Prohibition) gave us a glut of would-be brewers. After all, it seems natural to want to transform one's hobby and passion into a business. But beer brewing on the craft-brewing scale is somewhat different from home brewing, which in turn is different from what our ancestors did in early America—though the principles are the same. The essential ingredients are water, grain,

Essential Gear

Varieties of beer. Everyone knows about wine varieties, but few know that beer can be equally varied and complex. These are the four basic types of beer, first classified in the 1970s by the famous beer writer Michael Jackson. These types are *ale*, *lager*, *spontaneous fermentation*, and *hybrid*. The differences are created not only by choice of ingredients, but fermentation process. *Ale* is brewed with top-fermenting yeasts, usually at a higher temperature than lagers. This produces esters, which give a complex range of often fruity flavors and aromas. *Lagers*, from the German *lagern* ("to store"), are fermented at a cooler temperature and then stored (lagered) at around the freezing point. *Spontaneous fermentation* uses wild yeast, and is highly region-specific, since yeast flora flourish best in specific locations. Finally, *hybrids* may combine techniques, or add ingredients. For instance, *steam beers* use lager yeasts, but are fermented at ale temperatures.

A *pale ale* is a style of ale that uses pale malts and tends to have a light color. This is one of the most common styles of ale, known as "bitter" in Britain and *bière de garde* in France, and ranges from very hoppy to very fruity. *India pale ale* is a dry, very hoppy brew originally created to survive shipping to British troops in India. A *brown ale* is a British style that uses a darker barley malt. The roasting gives it a brown color and something of a nutty taste, with hints of chocolate or caramel. *Dark ales* such as *porter* and *stout* take this even further by roasting the grain.

Perhaps the best-known variety of lager is *pilsner*, originating in Pilsen in Bohemia. It uses paler malts, soft water, and high-quality hops. Many American manufacturers refer to their beer as "pilsners" regardless of hop character. *Pale lagers* also have a strong hop component and are pale; *Vienna lagers* use roasted grain and have a strong hop flavor, but are not fruity due to the lager-style fermentation process.

Lambics are the most commonly encountered type of spontaneously fermented type of beer. They are produced only in the Pajottenland region of Belgium, and use wild yeasts and bacteria indigenous to the Senne valley. This gives a lambic its distinctive taste—dry, cidery, and slightly sour.

and a fermenter. The grain (usually barley, but also wheat and rye) is simply boiled into something like a thick porridge; wild yeast or a starter from a previous batch ensures fermentation. The fermentable liquid created when the grain is boiled into a fermentable mixture is called the *wort*. Beginning in the late fourteenth century (though perhaps earlier or later, depending on region), the wort began to be boiled with hops, a flowering plant that both gives beer its distinctive flavor and acts as a preservative.

The winemaking process is different from brewing—simpler, in some ways, and more complex in others. Wine is the fermented juice (*must*) of crushed grapes. Red wine has the tannins and colorings of the skins of red grapes; white wine is made from white grapes or from red grapes where the skins are quickly removed from the must. Rosés are allowed to remain in contact with the skins for a short time. In the primary fermentation, yeasts convert most of the sugars in the juice into ethanol. In the secondary fermentation, the remainder of sugar is converted to ethanol in an airtight container. There are also variations: adding sugar or stopping the yeast from converting all of it to ethanol for a sweeter wine, or allowing additional fermentation in the bottle for Champagne and other sparkling wines.

So how does one learn these complex processes? Oenology, in keeping with wine's upper-crust image, is probably the more academic of the disciplines. It is possible to earn a bachelor's in oenology, and many of the degree programs are, unsurprisingly, in California. This is not to say that you need such a degree to become a vintner. If you have enough money, you can buy land, hire consultants, purchase equipment, and just learn by doing. Be forewarned: This is a costly and risky thing to do. Even a small vineyard takes millions of dollars to set up. The learning curve in the industry is steep, and you will have to know about many things besides making wine, from soil chemistry to distribution networks to labor laws. Profits are negligible, and you may operate at a loss for many years. In this respect, a winery is not much different from many other small businesses. However, it is also agricultural, meaning anything from bad weather to pests and diseases to labor shortages can go wrong before you even get the grapes pressed. The surest path to winemaking is education, then working for an established vineyard in roles of increasing responsibility. Look for academic programs, and, most importantly, for apprenticeships offered through schools, wineries, or trade organizations. Most vineyard owners are going to want you to have some experience before they will even think of hiring you.

Brewing, once a craft taught from master to apprentice, is rapidly becoming professionalized. Like wine, there is an established system of degree programs (many at agriculture-heavy public land-grant colleges) and apprenticeships both here an abroad. There are also online and other distance-learning courses available. Alternatively, you can find a job working at your local brewpub or microbrewery and learn the craft from the ground up. While opening your own brewery is an option, the equipment is expensive and significant profit eludes all but the most successful brewer. Though you do not have to worry about crop failures, the stress of running a business as you are trying to learn the trade of brewing may be too much to bear.

A final note about the Internet's effect on these industries: Though it seems like a good idea to sell your homemade beers and wines via your own Web site, many states' laws prohibit the sale of alcoholic beverages through the mail, or at least make it very difficult. For instance, you need to verify the receiver's age. Furthermore, many beers and wines do not travel well. Brewers and winemakers are thus better off working through established distributors or finding some way to self-distribute.

You Are Here

How to manage becoming a brewer or winemaker? Ask yourself these basic questions.

Do you have a background in chemistry, engineering, or another hard science? Brewing and winemaking have a lot in common with the sciences, and those with an analytical turn do well. A soil scientist is already ahead of the game when learning to become a vintner, and the processes used in brewing are not too dissimilar from what an industrial chemist or chemical engineer does every day. Career changers with these specialties may be able to transition smoothly—or even directly—into winemaking and brewing, or else through bridge jobs. For instance, a chemical engineer may start by engineering the production process, while a soil scientist may act as a consultant for a vineyard. The trick is learning the specific knowledge and the less quantitative, aesthetic qualities relating to brewing and winemaking.

Do you have a background in food? Like the potential brewer or winemaker with a background in the sciences, you are already ahead of the game, albeit from the other direction. You know about tastes, balancing flavors, and basic food chemistry. The aim now is to master the processes of beer or wine production. This requires both knowledge and experience. Look for educational programs, both online and at brick-and-mortar schools, and read all you can about the subject. Also look into home brewing or making wine at home so that you can see how the process works for yourself, and learn about the different varieties of beer and wine.

Are you up the river without a barrel? Not to worry. There are a lot of people out there who want to teach you winemaking or brewing—for a fee. Find programs near you (many are online distance-learning courses) and begin experimenting. An excellent way to start is by becoming a home brewer or home vintner. Basic kits can be inexpensive to buy, and in no time at all you can be producing in your own house. Also, learn as much about beer or wine as you can, whether by joining a tasting club, taking a class, or visiting brewpubs and wine bars and putting yourself in the hands of the masters.

Navigating the Terrain

I want to become a winemaker or brewer

Learn everything about beer or wine

Take courses and read up on the processes

Find an apprenticeship or entry-level job

Work your way up or start a business

Stories from the Field

Jim Koch
Brewer
Boston, Massachusetts

Despite being the owner and founder of the largest craft brewing company in America—the Boston Brewing Company—Jim Koch's business card says simply "brewer." Familiar to many as the voice in the Samuel Adams commercials, Koch is every bit true to his belief in quality beer as public image would suggest. "I never have to drink anything but good beer," as he told CNN in a 2001 interview.

Beer, you could say, is in Koch's blood. He is the sixth generation of his family to brew beer. But for a long time, it seemed, the Koch (pronounced "cook") dynasty was at an end. Koch's father was driven out of business by the American mass-brewing mega-corporations like Anheuser-Busch and Coors. Accordingly, he encouraged his son to go into another line of work. Koch's early career was eclectic. He graduated from Harvard in 1971 with a degree in government. After working for Outward Bound for three years (he is still an avid mountaineer), he returned for a JD from Harvard Law School and MBA from Harvard Business School. But Koch's first love was always beer, and so, in 1984, he decided to go back to his roots.

Organizing Your Expedition

Before you set out, know where you are going.

Decide on a destination. You have two basic choices that you can make in both brewing and winemaking: to start your own business or to try to find employment for someone else. The two are not mutually exclusive. It is a wise idea to work for someone else and learn the ropes before trying to make your own way. A mentor in the business world is an essential piece of gear.

Scout the terrain. There is no one right way to become a winemaker or brewer. The conventional path is to take academic courses or find an apprenticeship or both, either in the United States or in Europe. However,

Koch's strategy was not to compete with the big boys—it was to make something better. A recipe he took straight from his great-great grandfather became the first batch of Samuel Adams lager, named after the Revolutionary War-era patriot who was not only a Boston Tea Party participant but also a brewer. Koch worked tirelessly to promote his beer, giving free samples to Boston-area bartenders on the premise that if the bartenders liked it, they would recommend it to their customers. In 1985, Samuel Adams lager was named the best beer in the country at Denver Great American Beer Festival.

According to Koch, however, the keys to brewing success cannot be taught at Harvard. "You've got to have passion for beer, a good palate," as he told CNN. "You've got to be able to blend the science of beer with the art of what makes a great beer." Accordingly, during the Boston beer company's enormous growth throughout the last three decades, he has remained involved in all steps of production, from flying to Europe to choose the hops to tasting the finished product. The results have altered American brewing. Today Samuel Adams brews more than 18 varieties of beer with a total yearly production of over 1 million barrels.

because of your age, family situation, or finances, this may not be open to you. There are, however, many ways to learn both winemaking and brewing. Distance-learning, especially over the Internet, is becoming more and more popular. (See "Further Resources.")

Find the path that's right for you. No matter whether you take and academic or less traditional path toward your goal, the most important ingredient is experience. To this end, look to take a job in a winery or brewery. Considering that most towns have brewpubs and that there is a winery in every state, it is likely there is work someplace near you. Capitalize on your talents and abilities as much as possible in these bridge jobs—even if you start as the winery accountant, it is still a way into the world of wine or beer.

Landmarks

If you are in your twenties . . . Career changers of this age are the norm, though in the case of brewing or winemaking, you may find yourself the youngest of your peers. In the United States, many people come to these trades from other careers later in life. Be honest with yourself: Odds are that you have an undeveloped palate and very little experience. The good news is that this means you have plenty of time to learn and few accumulated errors to correct. Look for training programs, whether in the flesh or online, and, especially, gain as much experience as you can with different mentors.

If you are in your thirties or forties . . . Many people look to become brewers or winemakers at this stage of life. If you have the financial wherewithal, you can easily enter a training program and make the transition. However, you also have to be honest with yourself: Is this a true calling, or are you trying to escape from your workaday world? Brewing and winemaking are hard work, and you have no guarantee that you will find a job at the end of it.

If you are in your fifties . . . While it is entirely possible to become a brewer or winemaker at this stage of life, senior career changers may have difficulty finding apprenticeships and may resent having to take entry-level jobs (or be judged overqualified for them). This is the time when you might think about opening your own vineyard or brewery. However, much like the midcareer changer, you need to take stock of yourself and your motivations: Is this what you really want to do, or are you running away from something? The senior career changer has an additional challenge: with financial comfort comes the possibility of foolishly investing in real estate and equipment that you simply do not have the energy, wherewithal, knowledge, or business acumen with which to turn into a profit.

If you are over sixty . . . Many second-career starters who want to become brewers or winemakers have dreams of retiring to a sunny California vineyard, or perhaps running their own brewpub. Stop and take stock. Recognize that you may be throwing away your life savings chasing windmills (or wine presses, as the case might be). However, if you have the resources and keep your expectations low, there is no reason why you cannot make this work. Expertise (or at least the help of experts) can be hired. In this way, you might gain the satisfaction of making someone else's dream of becoming a brewer or winemaker come true.

Further Resources

MKF Wine industry statistics, industry research, and business advisors. An extremely useful site. http://www.mkf.org

Beertown.org Industry news and information for craft brewers. http://www.beertown.org

Brewery Age "The industry magazine for the brewing industry." http://www.breweryage.com

American Brewers Guild Offering online correspondence courses. http://www.abgbrew.com

Siebel Institute The preeminent institute of brewing education. http://www.siebelinstitute.com

Restaurant Reviewer or Food Critic

Restaurant Reviewer or Food Critic

Career Compasses

Here's the breakdown of what it takes to become a restaurant reviewer or food critic.

Relevant Knowledge of world cuisines and dining (20%)

Caring about fine cuisine (30%)

Communications Skills since being a good writer is essential (40%)

Organizational Skills to make deadlines and track receipts (10%)

Destination: Restaurant Reviewer or Food Critic

With the growth of the "foodie" movement and restaurant guides such as Zagat's, the job title of restaurant reviewer and food critic has shot into the limelight. Can any food-lover really think of a more desirable position? You get to go to the finest restaurants, order everything on the menu, and be paid for your efforts. The truth is that it is a very difficult field to break into. Besides the fact that it is probably the most coveted position in journalism, it is not as easy to do as you might think.

Essential Gear

History of the *Michelin Guide*. The *Michelin Guide* is the bible of restaurant reviews. In 1886 André Michelin, a Parisian engineer, took over his grandfather's agricultural goods and farm equipment business (which also sold vulcanized rubber products) and brought in his younger Édouard as managing director. The brothers found success in the 1890s selling a repairable bicycle tire of André's design, and quickly began manufacturing automobile tires when cars became popular. In 1900 André published the first edition of his guide to help motorists find lodging, food, gas, and supplies when taking off into the new frontier of the open road. The guide was distributed free until 1920, and in 1926 the Michelins started adding a star next to establishments with good cooking. In the early 1930s, they added two and three stars to denote truly excellent establishments. One star is "interesting," two stars is "worth a detour," and three stars is "worth a trip of its own." While Michelin does not give bad reviews (they simply will not mention the establishment), a good mention in Michelin can make a restaurant. However, very few restaurants of those mentioned get even one star; very, very few get two, and almost none get three: Out of Paris' 13,000 restaurants, only about 60 have three stars. Only 39 of New York City's 25,000 got even one star. Today, Michelin offers guides for 12 European countries and five cities outside Europe (New York, San Francisco, Tokyo, Los Angeles, and Las Vegas). Michelin claims to revisit restaurants every 18 months to note if there has been any change. They also note restaurants with good food at moderate prices.

The reviewer must be objective and consider the restaurant dispassionately and in line with established criteria.

First, the facts: Restaurant reviewers and food critics are people who write and publish about food. They work for newspapers, television stations, Web sites, and other media outlets. Most are in print, whether it is magazines, newspapers, the Web, or specialty guides. Some, such as the contributors to the Zagat guides or Chowhound.com, are simply consumers who are not reimbursed for their efforts; some are dedicated professional food critics; and some, especially in smaller markets, are regular reporters who also cover a food beat. In the latter case, the job is not just reviewing restaurants; you usually have to write other things, such as features and investigative pieces, as well. A restaurant reviewer or food critic might also have a hand in the editing and publishing aspects of the business.

While *restaurant reviewer* and *food critic* seem synonymous, important distinctions need to be made. The main difference between the two is that the restaurant reviewer concentrates on formal restaurants, with the French culinary experience being the gold standard. The restaurant reviewer looks not just at culinary excellence and how well the establishment conforms to the supposedly authoritative form set out by the French model, but also ambiance, service, and other aspects. Their bible and model is the French *Michelin Guide*, which introduced the "star" system of rating restaurants.

Food critics, on the other hand, have a broader, more contemporary spin, and thrive on the weird, the informal, the non-Western, and the everyday food experience. Thus, a food critic might do a roundup of the best hot dog places in the city, write a feature on which lunch truck has the best *tacos al pastor*, and categorize the finest five-star falafel purveyors. In the broader sense, food critics might not even review eateries at all, instead devoting pieces to produce, regional cuisine, or recipes. Shoehorning everything from dim sum to pierogi into the "objective" Michelin model of excellence (see "Essential Tools") is difficult. The food critic must be familiar with the conventions of each cuisine to rate it on its own merits.

Quantifying how much restaurant reviewers and food critics make is difficult. To begin with, many work freelance; in fact, there are few freelance writers in an urban area who have *not* contributed to a review or guide. However, they *are* writers and editors, and so the salaries of their colleagues in other media earn can be a guide. According to the U.S Bureau of Labor Statistics, the median earnings for news reporters and correspondents were $33,470 in 2006, with the middle 50 percent earning between $24,370 and $51,700, the lowest 10 percent earning less than $19,180, and the highest-paid 10 percent earning over $73,880. Those working in print media tend to be paid less. The median annual earnings for salaried writers and editors were $48,640, with the middle 50 percent earning between $34,850 and $67,820 and the highest 10 percent more than $97,700.

The most difficult thing about becoming a food critic or restaurant reviewer is that it is a job with no shortage of volunteers. With the advent of Web sites like Epicurious.com, Chowhound.com, and Mouthfuls.com, anyone can write up meals they have enjoyed or post new culinary discoveries. There are also countless food blogs, written by both culinary professionals and amateur connoisseurs. Your city may also have a number of city guides or weekly newspapers, each of which may pay freelance writers money for restaurant reviews. However, getting paid for writing about food and restaurants as a full-time job is much more difficult. Each magazine or newspaper can only have so many people on staff, and whether or not they can afford a full-time food critic or restaurant reviewer is highly variable. The *New York Times* can afford several because this is what its affluent readership demands, but this is not common among your average local weekly paper.

The qualifications for the job also set the bar quite high. To begin with, you need to be a good writer, with a long list of publication credits. You also need a long history of having written about food. Generally, this is not a career that one can prepare for through an established academic track, though taking cooking courses and having majored in English, communications, or journalism can help. Rather, many restaurant reviewers and food critics start out as journalists or writers, and then develop the food "beat" as their careers progress. Esteemed food critic R. W. Apple started as a reporter, while Ruth Reichl, the famous *New York Times* food critic, began in the West Coast counterculture scene as a chef in a collectively owned restaurant before becoming a food writer.

There are also less-specific qualifications for being a restaurant reviewer. For starters, you need to be an adventurous eater, lack prejudices, and be knowledgeable about food. While you may have been eating all your life, that does not mean you have an educated palate. Exactly how is *coq au vin* supposed to taste? When is pasta *al dente*, and when is it simply undercooked? Is pad thai supposed to have broccoli in it? How does the dish balance sweet and savory, richness and astringency? Does it keep with the cuisine's received traditions? All of these things require a careful culinary education and, more often than not, a degree of foreign travel. You also have to be able to relate sensory impressions through writing—a very difficult task. While restaurant reviewers may have a standard arsenal of descriptors, you have to break the confines of ordinary writing. Be creative! "The mole sauce, heavy on cilantro and chili, was hot enough to strip paint off a '69 Charger" is much more creative and specific than "The brown enchilada sauce was spicy." However, while avoiding cliché is essential, it is not enough. A creative turn of phrase, an apt simile, or clever wordplay delights the reader and differentiates the good writer from the merely competent.

You also have to be sensitive. Objectivity is paramount. You may think it is funny to use hyperbole to tell the readers how much you loved (or hated) the ma-po tofu, but it is as unprofessional to call its consistency "mucous-like" as it is to wax poetic about "a bouquet of complex flavors, redolent of the exoticism of the East and fit for an emperor." The former is insulting; the latter downright foolish, as ma-po tofu is a rather basic Szechuan comfort food. Finally, you have to be clear in your writing. Readers have to know exactly what you are talking about. Was the tempura too greasy, or was it the udon noodles? Was there too much cardamom in the sauce? And, of course, there is the basic knowledge of being able to identify what you are eating. Are you even sure it *was* cardamom? Having to ask the chef may lead to embarrassment!

Navigating the Terrain

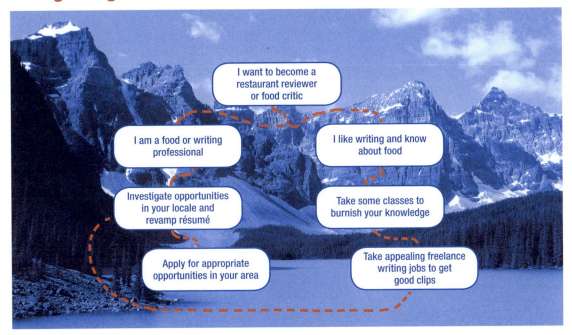

I want to become a restaurant reviewer or food critic

I am a food or writing professional

I like writing and know about food

Investigate opportunities in your locale and revamp résumé

Take some classes to burnish your knowledge

Apply for appropriate opportunities in your area

Take appealing freelance writing jobs to get good clips

Restaurant reviewers cannot like food *too* much, for several reasons. First, this is a career in which obesity is an occupational hazard. Secondly, you need to be an objective and careful judge of the flavor, texture, consistency, and preparation of each item, not simply cramming everything in your mouth. You cannot have a propensity for insanely spicy foods or for dumping mounds of Parmasean cheese on your pasta. You must take things as the chef makes them, and consider how a middle-of-the road eater would enjoy them. Impartiality is also key: You cannot be sentimental toward places where you are a regular or have a relationship with the owner, or give every deli in town a five-star rating because it reminds you of your mother's latkes.

Finally, the budding restaurant reviewer or food critic needs to recognize that people are going to disagree with his or her assessments. Restaurant-owners and chefs are particularly vocal about "amateur" reviewers' "unqualified" opinions. After all, bad reviews hurt their business, and a review from the Michelin guide or the *New York Times* can make or break a restaurant. However, you cannot please all the people all the time, and part of being a writer is learning to take criticism.

You Are Here

How does one become a restaurant reviewer or food critic?

Are you a journalist or other professional writer? This is probably the prime requisite for becoming a restaurant reviewer or food critic. As a professional writer, you not only know how to turn a snappy phrase, but you are also familiar with deadlines, journalistic objectivity, and how to work a "hook" into a story. Your task now is to get on the food "beat." Talk to your editors and work your network. If you are used to freelancing, you already know how to find new forms for your writing and make pitches. Build up a portfolio, and work your way up.

Are you a chef or other food professional? If you know food intimately, then you are ahead of the game. You have already seasoned your palate, and you have the critical vocabulary necessary to compose thoughtful reviews. Your task is now to sharpen your writing chops. Start by pitching articles and reviews to local newspapers and magazines. You may also

Notes from the Field

H. Q. Latimer Dodds
Food critic
New York, New York

What were you doing before you decided to change careers?

I was a securities analyst [makes a snoring noise]

Why did you change your career?

Quite simply, I'm passionate about food. I've always been one of those people who has to tell all their friends about their latest great restaurant experience, where to dine in Stuttgart, or about an amazing new tomato sauce, or where to buy fresh coriander. When I started thinking about changing careers it was an easy decision.

How did you make the transition?

I knew I was going to quit my job, so I saved up some money and did everything I had wanted to do when I was working but couldn't: a cooking class at the French Culinary Institute, dinner at the James Beard Foundation, taking a trip to Tuscany. I met contacts and had a friend at the neighborhood paper who gave me a weekly restaurant beat and it went on from there. I've never looked back.

What are the keys to success in your new career?

Communication. It is one thing to love food, wine, the good life, etc, but you need to be able to express yourself and make your feelings and thoughts important to the reader. Otherwise, you are just reviewing products.

want to start a food blog. Do not pass up opportunities to do other sorts of writing, as well. Your objective is to build up a strong enough portfolio that someone will give you a chance at writing about food full-time.

Are you merely a foodie? In this case, your task is harder. You need to become educated about fine cuisine—not merely a gourmand, but someone who understands and appreciates food in an educated way. You must comprehend how the orchestra works together, as it were, not merely how the conductor waves the baton. To this end, cooking courses and culinary education are invaluable. You also need to hone your writing skills. This is difficult, as writing is an art, not a science. Start a blog to develop your technique while reaching an audience, however limited. Look for freelance assignments to establish your credentials as a food writer. In time, you will build up enough of a portfolio to qualify for more regular assignments.

Organizing Your Expedition

Before you set out, know where you are going.

Decide on a destination. Becoming a restaurant reviewer or food critic means that you want to write about food. This requires two things: you need to know how to write, and you need to know about food. The first thing you need to do is take stock of your present abilities. Are you a published writer? A culinary professional? Address your weaknesses through reading, independent research, or simply talking to those already in the field.

Scout the terrain. If you do not feel that you have enough experience as a writer or a culinary expert, consider enrolling in writing courses, culinary courses, and pitching stories. A degree program is rarely necessary, but adult-education programs can help move you along. Also, look at your local market. Which newspapers and magazines publish articles on food or restaurant reviews? Are there local restaurant guides? Who writes for them, and do they take submissions? If their Web sites do not say, e-mail an editor and find out—at the very least, the contact is worth making.

Find the path that's right for you. Just because you do not have a previous background in writing or publishing does not mean that you cannot find success as a restaurant reviewer or food critic. Tim and Nina Zagat were lawyers before they founded their famous series of Zagat guides. Be creative! Perhaps there is a niche market that is not being met—a vegetarian review guide to your city? A guide to organic or small farms in New England? Remember that you not only have established print media outlets and Web sites, but also the Internet available to you. Note, however, that to make a living as a full-time restaurant reviewer or food critic is a rare thing; more likely (unless you are extraordinarily lucky), this will remain a pleasant sideline.

Landmarks

If you are in your twenties . . . At this age, you likely lack the experience to become a really effective restaurant reviewer or food critic. However, while you may have a way to go, but also have plenty of time to build your credentials. Build up your writing portfolio, both by writing about food and anything else you can. Educate your palate, read other food writers, and study the history of cuisine. Consider looking for a full-time job as a reporter or writer. By the time an opportunity comes along, you will be ready for it.

If you are in your thirties or forties . . . A midcareer changer with a history of writing and/or food industry jobs behind them is in a good place to transition to becoming a restaurant reviewer or food critic. If you cannot work your network to find an open position, then consider taking freelance assignments and pitching stories to build your portfolio. If you are not experienced, then you should start learning the ropes as soon as you can.

If you are in your fifties . . . This is when people who have been following this career path all along are becoming reviewers for prestigious publications, but becoming a restaurant reviewer or food critic is more difficult without a career behind you. If you do have the relevant experience, work your network. If not, there is no time like the present to get a start. Begin modestly by writing for your community paper, then branch out from there. Recognize, however, that at this point in your life your new career will more than likely remain a pleasant hobby or a sideline, not the main way in which you earn your living.

If you are over sixty . . . Much the same advice that goes for senior career changes goes for second-career starters. Start small, educate yourself, and bear in mind that the "big time" is very hard to reach. Either learn to be satisfied with food writing as a sideline, or if you do want to make this a real second career and you have the necessary experience, start your own publication or Web site.

Further Resources

Interview with Nina Zagat One of the Zagat Guide's founders discusses the company's genesis. http://www.slate.com/id/29583/entry/29585
Ruth Reichl Web site of the famous *New York Times* food writer. http://www.ruthreichl.com
Chowhound Amateur restaurant-review and food criticism Web site. http://www.chowhound.com
Epicurious Amateur restaurant-review and food criticism Web site. http://www.epicurious.com
Mouthfuls Amateur restaurant-review and food criticism Web site. http://www.mouthfuls.com

Appendix A

Going Solo: Starting Your Own Business

Starting your own business can be very rewarding—not only in terms of potential financial success, but also in the pleasure derived from building something from the ground up, contributing to the community, being your own boss, and feeling reasonably in control of your fate. However, business ownership carries its own obligations—both in terms of long hours of hard work and new financial and legal responsibilities. If you succeed in growing your business, your responsibilities only increase. Many new business owners come in expecting freedom only to find themselves chained tighter to their desks than ever before. Still, many business owners find greater satisfaction in their career paths than do workers employed by others.

The Internet has also changed the playing field for small business owners, making it easier than ever before to strike out on your own. While small mom-and-pop businesses such as hairdressers and grocery stores have always been part of the economic landscape, the Internet has made reaching and marketing to a niche easier and more profitable. This has made possible a boom in *microbusinesses*. Generally, a microbusiness is considered to have under ten employees. A microbusiness is also sometimes called a *SoHo* for "small office/home office."

The following appendix is intended to explain, in general terms, the steps in launching a small business, no matter whether it is selling your Web-design services or opening a pizzeria with business partners. It will also point out some of the things you will need to bear in mind. Remember also that the particular obligations of your municipality, state, province, or country may vary, and that this is by no means a substitute for doing your own legwork. Further suggested reading is listed at the end.

Crafting a Business Plan

It has often been said that success is 1 percent inspiration and 99 percent perspiration. However, the interface between the two can often be hard to achieve. The first step to taking your idea and making it reality is constructing a viable *business plan*. The purpose of a business plan is to think things all the way through, to make sure your ideas really are profitable, and to figure out the "who, what, when, where, why, and how" of your business. It fills in the details for three areas: your goals, why you think they are attainable, and how you plan to get to there. "You need to know where you're going before you take that first step," says Drew Curtis, successful Internet entrepreneur and founder of the popular newsfilter Fark.com.

Take care in writing your business plan. Generally, these documents contain several parts: An *executive summary* stating the essence of the plan; a *market summary* explaining how a need exists for the product and service you will supply and giving an idea of potential profitability by comparing your business to similar organizations; a *company description* which includes your products and services, why you think your organization will succeed, and any special advantages you have, as well as a description of *organization* and *management*; and your *marketing and sales strategy*. This last item should include market highlights and demographic information and trends that relate to your proposal. Also include a *funding request* for the amount of start-up capital you will need. This is supported by a section on *financials*, or the sort of cash flow you can expect, based on market analysis, projection, and comparison with existing companies. Other needed information, such as personal financial history, résumés, legal documents, or pictures of your product, can be placed in *appendices*.

Use your business plan to get an idea of how much startup money is necessary and to discipline your thinking and challenge your preconceived notions before you develop your cash flow. The business plan will tell you how long it will take before you turn a profit, which in turn is linked to how long it will before you will be able to pay back investors or a bank loan—which is something that anyone supplying you with money will want to know. Even if you are planning to subside on grants or you are not planning on investment or even starting a for-profit company, the discipline imposed by the business plan is still the first step to organizing your venture.

A business plan also gives you a realistic view of your personal financial obligations. How long can you afford to live without regular income? How are you going to afford medical insurance? When will your business begin turning a profit? How much of a profit? Will you need to reinvest your profits in the business, or can you begin living off of them? Proper planning is key to success in any venture.

A final note on business plans: Take into account realistic expected profit minus realistic costs. Many small business owners begin by underestimating start-ups and variable costs (such as electricity bills), and then underpricing their product. This effectively paints them into a corner from which it is hard to make a profit. Allow for realistic market conditions on both the supply and the demand side.

Partnering Up

You should think long and hard about the decision to go into business with a partner (or partners). Whereas other people can bring needed capital, expertise, and labor to a business, they can also be liabilities. The questions you need to ask yourself are:

☞ Will this person be a full and equal partner? In other words, are they able to carry their own weight? Make a full and fair assessment of your potential partner's personality. Going into business with someone who lacks a work ethic, or prefers giving directions to working in the trenches, can be a frustrating experience.

☞ What will they contribute to the business? For instance, a partner may bring in start-up money, facilities, or equipment. However, consider if this is enough of a reason to bring them on board. You may be able to get the same advantages in another way—for instance, renting a garage rather than working out of your partner's. Likewise, doubling skill sets does not always double productivity.

☞ Do they have any liabilities? For instance, if your prospective partner has declared bankruptcy in the past, this can hurt your collective venture's ability to get credit.

☞ Will the profits be able to sustain all the partners? Many start-up ventures do not turn profits immediately, and what little they do produce can be spread thin amongst many partners. Carefully work out the math.

Also bear in mind that going into business together can put a strain on even the best personal relationships. No matter whether it is family, friends, or strangers, keep everything very professional with written agreements regarding these investments. Get everything in writing, and be clear where obligations begin and end. "It's important to go into business with the right people," says Curtis. "If you don't—if it degrades into infighting and petty bickering—it can really go south quickly."

Incorporating. . . or Not

Think long and hard about incorporating. Starting a business often requires a fairly large—and risky—financial investment, which in turn exposes you to personal liability. Furthermore, as your business grows, so does your risk. Incorporating can help you shield yourself from this liability. However, it also has disadvantages.

To begin with, incorporating is not necessary for conducting professional transactions such as obtaining bank accounts and credit. You can do this as a sole proprietor, partnership, or simply by filing a DBA ("doing business as") statement with your local court (also known as "trading as" or an "assumed business name"). The DBA is an accounting entity that facilitates commerce and keeps your business' money separate from your own. However, the DBA does not shield you from responsibility if your business fails. It is entirely possible to ruin your credit, lose your house, and have your other assets seized in the unfortunate event of bankruptcy.

The purpose of incorporating is to shield yourself from personal financial liability. In case the worst happens, only the business' assets can be taken. However, this is not always the best solution. Check your local laws: Many states have laws that prevent a creditor from seizing a non-incorporated small business' assets in case of owner bankruptcy. If you are a corporation, however, the things you use to do business that are owned by the corporation—your office equipment, computers, restaurant refrigerators, and other essential equipment—may be seized by creditors, leaving you no way to work yourself out of debt. This is why it is imperative to consult with a lawyer.

There are other areas in which being a corporation can be an advantage, such as business insurance. Depending on your business needs, insurance can be for a variety of things: malpractice, against delivery failures or spoilage, or liability against defective products or accidents. Furthermore, it is easier to hire employees, obtain credit, and buy health insurance as an organization than as an individual. However, on the downside, corporations are subject to specific and strict laws concerning management and ownership. Again, you should consult with a knowledgeable legal expert.

Among the things you should discuss with your legal expert are the advantages and disadvantages of incorporating in your jurisdiction and which type of incorporation is best for you. The laws on liability and how much of your profit will be taken away in taxes vary widely by state and country. Generally, most small businesses owners opt for *limited liability companies* (LLCs), which gives them more control and a more flexible management structure. (Another possibility is a *limited liability partnership*, or *LLP*, which is especially useful for professionals such as doctors and lawyers.) Finally, there is the *corporation*, which is characterized by transferable ownerships shares, perpetual succession, and, of course, limited liability.

Most small businesses are sole proprietorships, partnerships, or privately-owned corporations. In the past, not many incorporated, since it was necessary to have multiple owners to start a corporation. However, this is changing, since it is now possible in many states for an individual to form a corporation. Note also that the form your business takes is usually not set in stone: A sole proprietorship or partnership can switch to become an LLC as it grows and the risks increase; furthermore, a successful LLC can raise capital by changing its structure to become a corporation and selling stock.

Legal Issues

Many other legal issues besides incorporating (or not) need to be addressed before you start your business. It is impossible to speak directly to every possible business need in this brief appendix, since regulations, licenses, and health and safety codes vary by industry and locality. A restaurant in Manhattan, for instance, has to deal not only with the usual issues such as health inspectors, the state liquor board, but obscure regulations such as New York City's cabaret laws, which prohibit dancing without a license in a place where alcohol is sold. An asbestos-abatement company, on the other hand, has a very different set of standards it has to abide by, including federal regulations. Researching applicable laws is part of starting up any business.

Part of being a wise business owner is knowing when you need help. There is software available for things like bookkeeping, business plans, and Web site creation, but generally, consulting with a knowledgeable professional—an accountant or a lawyer (or both)—is the smartest move. One of the most common mistakes is believing that just because you have expertise in the technical aspects of a certain field, you know all about running a business in that field. Whereas some people may balk at the expense, by suggesting the best way to deal with possible problems, as well as cutting through red tape and seeing possible pitfalls that you may not even have been aware of, such professionals usually more than make up for their cost. After all, they have far more experience at this than does a first-time business owner!

Financial

Another necessary first step in starting a business is obtaining a bank account. However, having the account is not as important as what you do with it. One of the most common problems with small businesses is undercapitalization—especially in brick-and-mortar businesses that sell or make something, rather than service-based businesses. The rule of thumb is that you should have access to money equal to your first year's anticipated profits, plus start-up expenses. (Note that this is not the same as having the money on hand—see the discussion on lines of credit, below.) For instance, if your annual rent, salaries, and equipment will cost $50,000 and you expect $25,000 worth of profit in your first year, you should have access to $75,000 worth of financing.

You need to decide what sort of financing you will need. Small business loans have both advantages and disadvantages. They can provide critical start-up credit, but in order to obtain one, your personal credit will need to be good, and you will, of course, have to pay them off with interest. In general, the more you and your partners put into the business yourselves, the more credit lenders will be willing to extend to you.

Equity can come from your own personal investment, either in cash or an equity loan on your home. You may also want to consider bringing on partners—at least limited financial partners—as a way to cover start-up costs.

It is also worth considering obtaining a line of credit instead of a loan. A loan is taken out all at once, but with a line of credit, you draw on the money as you need it. This both saves you interest payments and means that you have the money you need when you need it. Taking out too large of a loan can be worse than having no money at all! It just sits there collecting interest—or, worse, is spent on something utterly un-necessary—and then is not around when you need it most.

The first five years are the hardest for any business venture; your venture has about double the usual chance of closing in this time (1 out of 6, rather than 1 out of 12). You will probably have to tighten your belt at home, as well as work long hours and keep careful track of your business expenses. Be careful with your money. Do not take unnecessary risks, play it conservatively, and always keep some capital in reserve for emergencies. The hardest part of a new business, of course, is the learning curve of figuring out what, exactly, you need to do to make a profit, and so the best advice is to have plenty of savings—or a job to provide income—while you learn the ropes.

One thing you should not do is count on venture capitalists or "angel investors," that is, businesspeople who make a living investing on other businesses in the hopes that their equity in the company will increase in value. Venture capitalists have gotten something of a reputation as indiscriminate spendthrifts due to some poor choices made during the dot-com boom of the late 1990s, but the fact is that most do not take risks on unproven products. Rather, they are attracted to young companies that have the potential to become regional or national powerhouses and give better-than-average returns. Nor are venture capitalists are endless sources of money; rather, they are savvy businesspeople who are usually attracted to companies that have already experienced a measure of success. Therefore, it is better to rely on your own resources until you have proven your business will work.

Bookkeeping 101

The principles of double-entry bookkeeping have not changed much since its invention in the fifteenth century: one column records debits, and one records credits. The trick is *doing* it. As a small business owner, you need to be disciplined and meticulous at recording your finances. Thankfully, today there is software available that can do everything from tracking payables and receivables to running checks and generating reports.

Honestly ask yourself if you are the sort of person who does a good job keeping track of finances. If you are not, outsource to a bookkeeping company or hire someone to come in once or twice a week to enter invoices and generate checks for you. Also remember that if you have employees or even freelancers, you will have to file tax forms for them at the end of the year.

Another good idea is to have an accountant for your business to handle advice and taxes (federal, state, local, sales tax, etc.). In fact, consulting with an a certified public accountant is a good idea in general, since they are usually aware of laws and rules that you have never even heard of.

Finally, keep your personal and business accounting separate. If your business ever gets audited, the first thing the IRS looks for is personal expenses disguised as business expenses. A good accountant can help you to know what are legitimate business expenses. Everything you take from the business account, such as payroll and reimbursement, must be recorded and classified.

Being an Employer

Know your situation regarding employees. To begin with, if you have any employees, you will need an Employer Identification Number (EIN), also sometimes called a Federal Tax Identification Number. Getting an EIN is simple: You can fill out IRS form SS-4, or complete the process online at http://www.irs.gov.

Having employees carries other responsibilities and legalities with it. To begin with, you will need to pay payroll taxes (otherwise known as "withholding") to cover income tax, unemployment insurance, Social Security, and Medicare, as well as file W-2 and W-4 forms with the government. You will also be required to pay workman's compensation insurance, and will probably also want to find medical insurance. You are also required to abide by your state's nondiscrimination laws. Most states require you to post nondiscrimination and compensation notices in a public area.

Many employers are tempted to unofficially hire workers "off the books." This can have advantages, but can also mean entering a legal gray area. (Note, however, this is different from hiring freelancers, a temp employed by another company, or having a self-employed professional such as an accountant or bookkeeper come in occasionally to provide a service.) It is one thing to hire the neighbor's teenage son on a one-time basis to help you move some boxes, but quite another to have full-time workers working on a cash-and-carry basis. Regular wages must be noted in the accounts, and gaps may be questioned in the event of an audit. If the workers are injured on the job, you are not covered by workman's comp, and are thus vulnerable to lawsuits. If the workers you hired are not legal residents, you can also be liable for civil and criminal penalties. In general, it is best to keep your employees as above-board as possible.

Building a Business

Good business practices are essential to success. First off, do not overextend yourself. Be honest about what you can do and in what time frame. Secondly, be a responsible business owner. In general, if there is a problem, it is best to explain matters honestly to your clients than to leave them without word and wondering. In the former case, there is at least the possibility of salvaging your reputation and credibility.

Most business is still built by personal contacts and word of mouth. It is for this reason that maintaining your list of contacts is an essential practice. Even if a particular contact may not be useful at a particular moment, a future opportunity may present itself—or you may be able to send someone else to them. Networking, in other words, is as important when you are the boss as when you are looking for a job yourself. As the owner of a company, having a network means getting services on better terms, knowing where to go if you need help with a particular problem, or simply being in the right place at the right time to exploit an opportunity. Join professional organizations, the local Chamber of Commerce, clubs and community organizations, and learn to play golf. And remember—never burn a bridge.

Advertising is another way to build a business. Planning an ad campaign is not as difficult as you might think: You probably already know your media market and business community. The trick is applying it. Again, go with your instincts. If you never look twice at your local weekly, other people probably do not, either. If you are in a high-tourist area, though, local tourists maps might be a good way to leverage your marketing dollar. Ask other people in your area or market who have business similar to your own. Depending on your focus, you might want to consider everything from AM radio or local TV networks, to national trade publications, to hiring a PR firm for an all-out blitz. By thinking about these questions, you can spend your advertising dollars most effectively.

Nor should you underestimate the power of using the Internet to build your business. It is a very powerful tool for small businesses, potentially reaching vast numbers of people for relatively little outlay of money. Launching a Web site has become the modern equivalent of hanging out your shingle. Even if you are primarily a brick-and-mortar business, a Web presence can still be an invaluable tool—your store or offices will show up on Google searches, plus customers can find directions to visit you in person. Furthermore, the Internet offers the small-business owner many useful tools. Print and design services, order fulfillment, credit card processing, and networking—both personal and in terms of linking to other sites—are all available online. Web advertising can be useful, too, either by advertising on specialty sites that appeal to your audience, or by using services such as Google AdWords.

Amateurish print ads, TV commercials, and Web sites do not speak well of your business. Good media should be well-designed, well-edited, and well-put together. It need not, however, be expensive. Shop around and, again, use your network.

Flexibility is also important. "In general, a business must adapt to changing conditions, find new customers and find new products or services that customers need when the demand for their older products or services diminishes," says James Peck, a Long Island, New York, entrepreneur. In other words, if your original plan is not working out, or if demand falls, see if you can parlay your experience, skills, and physical plant into meeting other needs. People are not the only ones who can change their path in life; organizations can, too.

A Final Word

In business, as in other areas of life, the advice of more experienced people is essential. "I think it really takes three businesses until you know what you're doing," Drew Curtis confides. "I sure didn't know what I was doing the first time." Listen to what others have to say, no matter whether it is about your Web site or your business plan. One possible solution is seeking out a mentor, someone who has previously launched a successful venture in this field. In any case, before taking any step, ask as many people as many questions as you can. Good advice is invaluable.

Further Resources

American Independent Business Alliance
http://www.amiba.net

American Small Business League
http://www.asbl.com

IRS Small Business and Self-Employed One-Stop Resource
http://www.irs.gov/businesses/small/index.html

The Riley Guide: Steps in Starting Your Own Business
http://www.rileyguide.com/steps.html

Small Business Administration
http://www.sba.gov

Appendix B

Outfitting Yourself for Career Success

As you contemplate a career shift, the first component is to assess your interests. You need to figure out what makes you tick, since there is a far greater chance that you will enjoy and succeed in a career that taps into your passions, inclinations, natural abilities, and training. If you have a general idea of what your interests are, you at least know in which direction you want to travel. You may know you want to simply switch from one sort of nursing to another, or change your life entirely and pursue a dream you have always held. In this case, you can use a specific volume of The Field Guides to Finding a New Career to discover which position to target. If you are unsure of your direction you want to take, well, then the entire scope of the series is open to you! Browse through to see what appeals to you, and see if it matches with your experience and abilities.

The next step you should take is to make a list—do it once in writing—of the skills you have used in a position of responsibility that transfer to the field you are entering. People in charge of interviewing and hiring may well understand that the skills they are looking for in a new hire are used in other fields, but you must spell it out. Most job descriptions are partly a list of skills. Map your experience into that, and very early in your contacts with a prospective employer explicitly address how you acquired your relevant skills. Pick a relatively unimportant aspect of the job to be your ready answer for where you would look forward to learning within the organization, if this seems essentially correct. When you transfer into a field, softly acknowledge a weakness while relating your readiness to learn, but never lose sight of the value you offer both in your abilities and in the freshness of your perspective.

Energy and Experience

The second component in career-switching success is energy. When Jim Fulmer was 61, he found himself forced to close his piano-repair business. However, he was able to parlay his knowledge of music, pianos, and the musical instruments industry into another job as a sales representative for a large piano manufacturer, and quickly built up a clientele of

111

musical-instrument retailers throughout the East Coast. Fulmer's experience highlights another essential lesson for career-changers: There are plenty of opportunities out there, but jobs will not come to you—especially the career-oriented, well-paying ones. You have to seek them out.

Jim Fulmer's case also illustrates another important point: Former training and experience can be a key to success. "Anyone who has to make a career change in any stage of life has to look at what skills they have acquired but may not be aware of," he says. After all, people can more easily change into careers similar to the ones they are leaving. Training and experience also let you enter with a greater level of seniority, provided you have the other necessary qualifications. For instance, a nurse who is already experienced with administering drugs and their benefits and drawbacks, and who is also graced with the personality and charisma to work with the public, can become a pharmaceutical company sales representative.

Unlock Your Network

The next step toward unlocking the perfect job is networking. The term may be overused, but the idea is as old as civilization. More than other animals, humans need one another. With the Internet and telephone, never in history has it been easier to form (or revive) these essential links. One does not have to gird oneself and attend reunion-type events (though for many this is a fine tactic)—but keep open to opportunities to meet people who may be friendly to you in your field. Ben Franklin understood the principal well—*Poor Richard's Almanac* is something of a treatise on the importance or cultivating what Franklin called "friendships" with benefactors. So follow in the steps of the founding fathers and make friends to get ahead. Remember: helping others feels good; it's often the receiving that gets a little tricky. If you know someone particularly well-connected in your field, consider tapping one or two less important connections first so that you make the most of the important one. As you proceed, keep your strengths foremost in your mind because the glue of commerce is mutual interest.

Eighty percent of job openings are *never advertised*, and, according to the U.S. Bureau of Labor statistics, more than half all employees landed their jobs through networking. Using your personal contacts is far more efficient and effective than trusting your résumé to the Web. On the Web, an employer needs to sort through tens of thousands—or millions—of résumés. When you direct your application to one potential employer, you are directing your inquiry to one person who already knows you. The personal touch is everything: Human beings are social animals, programmed to "read" body language; we are naturally inclined to trust those we meet in person, or who our friends and coworkers have recommended. While Web sites can be useful (for looking through help-wanted ads, for instance), expecting employers to pick you out of the slush pile is as effective as throwing your résumé into a black hole.

Do not send your résumé out just to make yourself feel like you're doing something. The proper way to go about things is to employ discipline and order, and then to apply your charm. Begin your networking efforts by making a list of people you can talk to: colleagues, coworkers, and supervisors, people you have had working relationship with, people from church, athletic teams, political organizations, or other community groups, friends, and relatives. You can expand your networking opportunities by following the suggestions in each chapter of the volumes. Your goal here is not so much to land a job as to expand your possibilities and knowledge: Though the people on your list may not be in the position to help you themselves, they might know someone who is. Meeting with them might also help you understand traits that matter and skills that are valued in the field in which you are interested. Even if the person is a potential employer, it is best to phrase your request as if you were seeking information: "You might not be able to help me, but do you know someone I could talk to who could tell me more about what it is like to work in this field?" Being hungry gives one impression, being desperate quite another.

Keep in mind that networking is a two-way street. If you meet someone who had an opening that is not right for you, but if you could recommend someone else, you have just added to your list two people who will be favorably disposed toward you in the future. Also, bear in mind that *you* can help people in *your* old field, thus adding to your own contacts list.

Networking is especially important to the self-employed or those who start their own businesses. Many people in this situation begin because they either recognize a potential market in a field that they are familiar with, or because full-time employment in this industry is no longer a possibility. Already being well-established in a field can help, but so can asking connections for potential work and generally making it known that you are ready, willing, and able to work. Working your professional connections, in many cases, is the *only* way to establish yourself. A freelancer's network, in many cases, is like a spider's web. The spider casts out many strands, since he or she never knows which one might land the next meal.

Dial-Up Help

In general, it is better to call contacts directly than to e-mail them. E-mails are easy for busy people to ignore or overlook, even if they do not mean to. Explain your situation as briefly as possible (see the discussion of the "elevator speech"), and ask if you could meet briefly, either at their office or at a neutral place such as a café. (Be sure that you pay the bill in such a situation—it is a way of showing you appreciate their time and effort.) If you get someone's voicemail, give your "elevator speech" and then say you will call back in a few days to follow up—and then do so. If you reach your contact directly and they are too busy to speak or meet with you, make a definite appointment to call back at a later date. Be persistent, but not annoying.

Once you have arranged a meeting, prep yourself. Look at industry publications both in print and online, as well as news reports (here, GoogleNews, which lets you search through online news reports, can be very handy). Having up-to-date information on industry trends shows that you are dedicated, knowledgeable, and focused. Having specific questions on employers and requests for suggestions will set you apart from the rest of the job-hunting pack. Knowing the score—for instance, asking about the value of one sort of certification instead of another—pegs you as an "insider," rather than a dilettante, someone whose name is worth remembering and passing along to a potential employer.

Finally, set the right mood. Here, a little self-hypnosis goes a long way: Look at yourself in the mirror, and tell yourself that you are an enthusiastic, committed professional. Mood affects confidence and performance. Discipline your mind so you keep your perspective and self-respect. Nobody wants to hire someone who comes across as insincere, tells a sob story, or is still in the doldrums of having lost their previous job. At the end of any networking meeting, ask for someone else who might be able to help you in your journey to finding a position in this field, either with information or a potential job opening.

Get a Lift

When you meet with a contact in person (as well as when you run into anyone by chance who may be able to help you), you need an "elevator speech" (so-named because it should be short enough to be delivered during an elevator ride from a ground level to a high floor). This is a summary in which, in less than two minutes, you give them a clear impression of who you are, where you come from, your experience and goals, and why you are on the path you are on. The motto above Plato's Academy holds true: Know Thyself (this is where our Career Compasses and guides will help you). A long and rambling "elevator story" will get you nowhere. Furthermore, be positive: Neither a sad-sack story nor a tirade explaining how everything that went wrong in your old job is someone else's fault will get you anywhere. However, an honest explanation of a less-than-fortunate circumstance, such as a decline in business forcing an office closing, needing to change residence to a place where you are not qualified to work in order to further your spouse's career, or needing to work fewer hours in order to care for an ailing family member, is only honest.

An elevator speech should show 1) you know the business involved; 2) you know the company; 3) you are qualified (here, try to relate your education and work experience to the new situation); and 4) you are goal-oriented, dependable, and hardworking. Striking a balance is important; you want to sound eager, but not overeager. You also want to show a steady work experience, but not that you have been so narrowly focused that you cannot adjust. Most important is emphasizing what you can do for the company. You will be surprised how much information you can include in two minutes. Practice this speech in front of a mirror until you have the key points down perfectly. It should sound natural, and you should come across as friendly, confident, and assertive. Finally, remember eye contact! Good eye contact needs to be part of your presentation, as well as your everyday approach when meeting potential employers and leads.

Get Your Résumé Ready

Everyone knows what a résumé is, but how many of us have really thought about how to put one together? Perhaps no single part of the job search is subject to more anxiety—or myths and misunderstandings—than this 8 ½-by-11-inch sheet of paper.

On the one hand, it is perfectly all right for someone—especially in certain careers, such as academia—to have a résumé that is more than one page. On the other hand, you do not need to tell a future employer *everything*. Trim things down to the most relevant; for a 40-year-old to mention an internship from two decades ago is superfluous. Likewise, do not include irrelevant jobs, lest you seem like a professional career-changer.

Tailor your descriptions of your former employment to the particular position you are seeking. This is not to say you should lie, but do make your experience more appealing. If the job you're looking for involves supervising other people, say if you have done this in the past; if it involves specific knowledge or capabilities, mention that you possess these qualities. In general, try to make your past experience seem as similar to what you are seeking.

The standard advice is to put your Job Objective at the heading of the résumé. An alternative to this is a Professional Summary, which some recruiters and employers prefer. The difference is that a Job Objective mentions the position you are seeking, whereas a Professional Summary mentions your background (e.g. "Objective: To find a position as a sales representative in agribusiness machinery" versus "Experienced sales representative; strengths include background in agribusiness, as well as building team dynamics and market expansion"). Of course, it is easy to come up with two or three versions of the same document for different audiences.

The body of the résumé of an experienced worker varies a lot more than it does at the beginning of your career. You need not put your education or your job experience first; rather, your résumé should emphasize your strengths. If you have a master's degree in a related field, that might want to go before your unrelated job experience. Conversely, if too much education will harm you, you might want to bury that under the section on professional presentations you have given that show how good you are at communicating. If you are currently enrolled in a course or other professional development, be sure to note this (as well as your date of expected graduation). A résumé is a study of blurs, highlights, and jewels. You blur everything you must in order to fit the description of your experience to the job posting. You highlight what is relevant from each and any of your positions worth mentioning. The jewels are the little headers and such—craft them, since they are what is seen first.

You may also want to include professional organizations, work-related achievements, and special abilities, such as your fluency in a foreign language. Also mention your computer software qualifications and capabilities, especially if you are looking for work in a technological field or if you are an older job-seeker who might be perceived as behind the technology curve. Including your interests or family information might or might not be a good idea—no one really cares about your bridge club, and in fact they might worry that your marathon training might take away from your work commitments, but, on the other hand, mentioning your golf handicap or three children might be a good idea if your potential employer is an avid golfer or is a family woman herself.

You can either include your references or simply note, "References available upon request." However, be sure to ask your references' permission to use their names and alert them to the fact that they may be contacted before you include them on your résumé! Be sure to include name, organization, phone number, and e-mail address for each contact.

Today, word processors make it easy to format your résumé. However, beware of prepackaged résumé "wizards"—they do not make you stand out in the crowd. Feel free to strike out on your own, but remember the most important thing in formatting a résumé is consistency. Unless you have a background in typography, do not get too fancy. Finally, be sure to have someone (or several people!) read your résumé over for you.

For more information on résumé writing, check out Web sites such as http://www.resume.monster.com.

Craft Your Cover Letter

It is appropriate to include a cover letter with your résumé. A cover letter lets you convey extra information about yourself that does not fit or is not always appropriate in your résumé, such as why you are no longer working in your original field of employment. You can and should also mention the name of anyone who referred you to the job. You can go into some detail about the reason you are a great match, given the job description. Also address any questions that might be raised in the potential employer's mind (for instance, a gap in employment). Do not, however, ramble on. Your cover letter should stay focused on your goal: To offer a strong, positive impression of yourself and persuade the hiring manager that you are worth an interview. Your cover letter gives you a chance to stand out from the other applicants and sell yourself. In fact, according to a CareerBuilder.com survey, 23 percent of hiring managers say a candidate's ability to relate his or her experience to the job at hand is a top hiring consideration.

Even if you are not a great writer, you can still craft a positive yet concise cover letter in three paragraphs: An introduction containing the specifics of the job you are applying for; a summary of why you are a good fit for the position and what you can do for the company; and a closing with a request for an interview, contact information, and thanks. Remember to vary the structure and tone of your cover letter—do not begin every sentence with "I."

Ace Your Interview

In truth, your interview begins well before you arrive. Be sure to have read up well on the company and its industry. Use Web sites and magazines—http://www.hoovers.com offers free basic business information, and trade magazines deliver both information and a feel for the industries they cover. Also, do not neglect talking to people in your circle who might know about trends in the field. Leave enough time to digest the information so that you can give some independent thought to the company's history and prospects. You don't need to expert when you arrive to be interviewed; but you should be comfortable. The most important element of all is to be poised and relaxed during the interview itself. Preparation and practice can help a lot.

Be sure to develop well-thought-through answers to the following, typical interview openers and standard questsions.

☞ Tell me about yourself. (Do not complain about how unsatisfied you were in your former career, but give a brief summary

of your applicable background and interest in the particular job area.) If there is a basis to it, emphasize how much
you love to work and how you are a team player.

☞ Why do you want this job? (Speak from the brain, and the heart—of
course you want the money, but say a little here about what you
find interesting about the field and the company's role in it.)

☞ What makes you a good hire? (Remember here to connect the
company's needs and your skill set. Ultimately, your selling
points probably come down to one thing: you will make your employer money. You want the prospective hirer to see that your
skills are valuable not to the world in general but to this specific company's bottom line. What can you do for them?)

☞ What led you to leave your last job? (If you were fired, still try say
something positive, such as, "The business went through a challenging time, and some of the junior marketing people were let go.")

Practice answering these and other questions, and try to be genuinely positive about yourself, and patient with the process. Be secure but
not cocky; don't be shy about forcing the focus now and then on positive
contributions you have made in your working life—just be specific. As
with the elevator speech, practice in front of the mirror.

A couple pleasantries are as natural a way as any to start the actual
interview, but observe the interviewer closely for any cues to fall silent
and formally begin. Answer directly; when in doubt, finish your phrase
and look to the interviewer. Without taking command, you can always
ask, "Is there more you would like to know?" Your attentiveness will convey respect. Let your personality show too—a positive attitude and a
grounded sense of your abilities will go a long way to getting you considered. During the interview, keep your cell phone off and do not look at
your watch. Toward the end of your meeting, you may be asked whether
you have any questions. It is a good idea to have one or two in mind. A
few examples follow:

☞ "What makes your company special in the field?"
☞ "What do you consider the hardest part of this position?"
☞ "Where are your greatest opportunities for growth?"
☞ "Do you know when you might need anything further from me?"

Leave discussion of terms for future conversations. Make a cordial, smooth exit.

Remember to Follow Up

Send a thank-you note. Employers surveyed by CareerBuilder.com in 2005 said it matters. About 15 percent said they would not hire someone who did not follow up with a thanks. And almost 33 percent would think less of a candidate. The form of the note does not much matter—if you know a manager's preference, use it. Otherwise, just be sure to follow up.

Winning an Offer

A job offer can feel like the culmination of a long and difficult struggle. So naturally, when you hear them, you may be tempted to jump at the offer. Don't. Once an employer wants you, he or she will usually give you a chance to consider the offer. This is the time to discuss terms of employment, such as vacation, overtime, and benefits. A little effort now can be well worth it in the future. Be sure to do a check of prevailing salaries for your field and area before signing on. Web sites for this include Payscale.com, Salary.com, and Salaryexpert.com. If you are thinking about asking for better or different terms from what the prospective employer offered, rest assured—that's how business gets done; and it may just burnish the positive impression you have already made.

Index